# The Day He Was Gone

Anjum Awasthi Malik

Invincible Publishers

First published in India in 2018

©2018 Anjum Awasthi Malik, All Rights Reserved

ISBN: 978-93-88333-03-0

No part of this publication may be reproduced or stored in a retrieval system, or transmitted in any form or by any means, electronic, mechanical, photocopying, recording or otherwise, without the prior permission of the publishers.

Invincible Publishers

G-120, Sushant Lok III, Sector 57, Gurgaon-122002

Registered Address: Opposite Kasturba Ashram, Radaur, Haryana–135133

*Dedicated to all my readers*
*(I wouldn't have done it otherwise)*

# Prologue

**9 June, 2012**

The car made a screeching sound as the driver hit the brakes outside the hotel. She clambered off the car and looked at the magnificent entrance of the hotel, ***The Grand Rajvilaas.*** She waddled through the hotel corridor, holding a large bouquet of roses and tucking her head down. All she wanted was to not get noticed by anyone, yet she was there, having come to attend the engagement party of her best friend. She had been avoiding going out since that fateful day. She wouldn't have appeared that day either if it weren't for her best friend. Her friend had insisted incessantly for her to attend her engagement party. She headed straight for the elevator and pushed the call button. She kept her gaze down as a couple emerged from the elevator. She stepped into it and heaved a sigh of relieve, finding herself alone inside. As the door closed, she turned to look at her reflection in the mirror mounted on the elevator wall.

'*Don't you feel ashamed when you look at yourself in the mirror? Girls like you should die in the womb of their mothers.*' The words ricocheted in her head and pierced her chest with a fiery pain.

Damn tears again!

She had been shedding a lot of tears lately, and she hated herself for it. She forced a smile on her face to blink away the uninvited tears, but instead, her body shook and she sniveled. She dabbed a handkerchief on her cheek to wipe off the moisture. A beep from the elevator made her aware of her arrival on the 14th floor of the building. She stepped off it and headed straight towards the function hall. The smell of fresh flowers hit her senses right away as she walked in. The lobby was beautifully decorated with flowers and colorful meshes, but nothing could bait her wounded heart.

She didn't bother to make eye contact or greet anyone, and padded straight towards her friend. She had decided that she would leave after wishing the couple. As soon as her friend noticed her approaching, she opened her arms to draw her into a tight hug.

"I am so glad to see you here. Despite such a tragedy in your family, you still came. I am so sorry to hear about your grandfather," her friend consoled her.

"It's okay. I am fine now," she said and forced a smile on her face before adding, "And I am so happy for both of you. I am sorry I couldn't bring anything for you," she said, handing over the bouquet to the couple.

"Don't worry, you can still make up for not bringing a gift?" her friend said, smiling.

"Anything for you."

"Go to the terrace. Something is waiting for you there. And I am not going to take 'no' for an answer," her friend said with a sly smile on her face.

"And what's there?"

"Just go. You will love the surprise," her friend urged, clutching her by her shoulders.

She nodded quietly in response. She knew that there was no use arguing with her friend. Besides, she was happy to keep herself away from this hullabaloo. She walked out of the hall almost immediately. Not considering her friend's request, she pushed the call button of the elevator to go down and head straight back home. But the few seconds that the elevator took to arrive at her floor changed her mind and she decided to go up instead. She took the stairs at the final floor to reach the terrace of the building. Little did she know that she wasn't just heading towards the top of the building, but to her end too.

A few incidents happen in our life that alter us in a way that it seems like a reincarnation, and this incident was one of those kind. Perhaps if she hadn't taken those stairs that day, the story would have been entirely different.

# 1

*Four years later*

"I can't believe how fortunate Reeva is! Otherwise, who gets such a splendid marriage proposal, that too without any effort?"

Reeva glared at her mother angrily, while her father nodded.

"Money is not everything, Maa. Other things matter too," Reeva said, looking down and twirling the spoon through the *Poha* on her plate. She had hardly eaten anything. This sudden marriage proposal from a hotel magnate had taken her off guard.

"I agree," her father supported her, "But you have to agree to this too, Reeva. He is a self-made man. Despite the empire his father had left for him, he carved his own way to success."

This was the thing that had been bothering Reeva ever since she had received that marriage proposal. Why did a magnate like him want to marry her? Why was he so interested in her when he could get the finest girl in the city? And how did he even find her? There was no common connection between them. There were so many questions in her mind and no one to answer them. It incessantly bugged her mind and wrecked her inner peace. His money had undoubtedly blinded her parents, but not her.

"A penny for your thoughts, Reeva," her father broke her trance.

"Why me, Daddy?" she poured out her mind in just two simple words, *why me?* Reeva was an ordinary girl with average looks and height. She wasn't rich like him, not even one-thousandth of what the guy was. Then, why her?

"Why not you? You are undermining your worth, *beta,*" her father said.

"That's not what I mean, Daddy." She paused for a moment to shape her thoughts into the words and then said, "He hasn't even seen me, and the way he has sent the proposal seems like he is determined to make this relationship happen. Otherwise, who sends diamond bangles worth a fortune just for fixing a date to meet?"

"Your luck has finally come knocking at your door, my girl. Don't take so much time to open it now," her mother said, pointing a spoon at her. "And how are you so sure that he has never seen you? Maybe he has, since you both live in the same city," she continued.

"That's not true. He comes here only once in a while to look after his father's business. He left Surat long back and is now settled in Mumbai," Reeva countered.

"So? That doesn't mean he doesn't belong to this city. Moreover, he will keep you like a queen. Just say *yes* and meet him once," her mother urged.

"Whatever. I'll have to think about it. I can't say 'yes' just because he is rich and owns a chain of luxury hotels."

"That is not a small thing. Look at us. It has been twenty-six years now and we are still hopping from one rented flat to another," her mother said.

Reeva's mother, Sumitra Panchal, had always wanted a house of her own, but the loan that her husband, Prakash Panchal, had taken for the treatment of his father had never let it happen. Prakash, Reeva's father, worked as an accountant in private industry. His salary would have been just enough to give them a decent life in a city like Surat, had he not been compelled to arrange funds for his father's treatment. Every month, half of his salary went as instalment to repay the loan he had taken.

Four years ago, Reeva had started her first job at a call-center, but soon realized that she would never be able to help her family with just that job. She had always been good at arts and crafts. So, she carved a niche for herself and started selling her paintings and handmade accessories online. As the earnings from her business rose, she resigned from her call-center job and started nourishing her business full-time. In no time, she had more than thirty thousand followers on her promotional page '*Kreative Krafts*' and hundreds of loyal customers too. She now owned a small office and a workshop where she worked with five other artisans. Her business was growing day by day, and she was proud of it, but her parents weren't satisfied with her choice of career and kept ranting about the same.

"Can you please stop being my mom for some time and try to understand my perspective like a friend?" Reeva couldn't quell the exasperation in her voice.

"Go on. I am in friend mode now," her mother said, wrapping up the breakfast and picking up bowls and plates from the table.

"One, he is eight years older than I am," Reeva said, scanning his biodata.

"There is a nine-year difference between your father and I," her mother retorted.

"Two, he owns a lot of property."

"Good for you, because the one I'm married to doesn't even own a tent." Reeva snickered at her mother's jibe.

"Three, his daily income is more than Daddy's yearly," Reeva continued, staring at the wide figure written against 'Income'.

"I am all green-eyed," her mother snorted. Prakash's gaze kept darting between his wife and his daughter.

"I know you both are doing it deliberately, but will you please stop comparing me with him?" her father intervened and both the ladies laughed.

"Four, he is too good-looking," Reeva said, looking back at the biodata and scrutinizing the photograph attached to it. Even though it was just a passport sized photograph, it couldn't suppress his captivating personality. His deep hazel eyes gleamed with a sense of self-reliance. His neatly trimmed stubble enhanced his chiseled jawline. His lush black hair were groomed to perfection and harmonized well with his wheatish complexion.

"That's an added advantage, isn't it?" Her mother's voice hauled her out of her daze.

"You don't get it, Maa. You have an answer to everything I say. But try to be in my shoes once."

"There must be thousands of girls who would kill to be in your shoes right now," her mother countered, wiping her hands on a towel. "You shouldn't think twice about such a magnificent proposal, Reeva. You are twenty-four already."

"Twenty three!"

"Whatever."

"I am not against getting married. It's just that I'm not sure about this guy. It all seems too good to be true, like a fairytale," Reeva said, shoving his biodata aside. She rose from her chair and strolled toward her room.

“Where are you going?” asked her mother.

“To the workshop, need to finish some pending work there,” she answered carelessly, without looking back at her mother.

“You can’t go anywhere today. You know he is coming to meet you in the evening,” Sumitra said, tailing Reeva to her room.

“I will be back by then. Don’t worry,” Reeva said, stuffing her handbag with the essentials.

“You will be exhausted by the evening. A girl must look fresh and well groomed on her first meeting, Reeva.”

“Maa, you know that I can’t compromise with my work,” peeved Reeva, coming out of her room.

“Ah! Your work! This is another topic we need to discuss in detail,” Sumitra said indignantly, and Reeva rolled her eyes in response. Whenever this topic popped up, she preferred to run rather than stay and discuss. Reeva knew that this topic would take her to the place she had been trying to avoid for long; a part of her life, she wished every day, had never happened. She paced towards the living room in an attempt to avoid the discussion.

“Well, it’s Sunday,” her father said loudly from behind, looking over his spectacles. Unlike Sumitra, Prakash never judged Reeva by her choices. He was more concerned about Reeva’s happiness and always supported her in all her decisions, while Sumitra was more concerned with the society. And someone opting for a small-scale business over a 9 to 5 job was considered a chump in the community, especially if it is a girl.

“You know there are only two options when it comes to dreams, you either put your everything into it or just forget about it, and I have decided to go with the former,” said Reeva, tying the laces of her shoes. “Moreover, this concept of a weekend is only for employees; owners don't get any holidays," she added haughtily as she stood up and adjusted the strap of her sling bag over her shoulder.

"By the way, I have an offer for you too. I am soon going to hire an accountant. You can apply for the post. An application form will be available on my website very soon," she winked at her father and giggled, just to make the air light. He shook his head in response and laughed.

"This business of yours is never going to grow, no matter how much effort you put in. I can give this to you in writing. Stop wasting your time over this and start doing something useful. I've told you this before too. Pandit ji clearly mentioned that anything that starts with a 'K' is ominous for you. But you have sworn not to listen to me and deliberately named your business from the letter 'K'," Sumitra fumed, her voice sounding so portentous to Reeva's ears that she quickened to pick up her things and rush out of the house, dreading that she would otherwise say something that she would repent later. She lived and breathed her work, and someone calling it ominous was painful to her ears.

Reeva left her home, banging the door behind her, and was soon on the road that led to her workshop. She preferred to walk instead of taking an auto. She weaved her way on foot through the morning rush; most of them were out walking their dogs. As she turned around the corner, she dropped a few coins in the pail of an old man sitting on the wayside with his hands joined. She was against begging, but could never stop herself at the sight of an old or disabled person.

Soon, she reached her workshop, unlocked the door and bowed before entering. This place was her temple, and her art her worship. Her workshop wasn't spacious, but just enough for her current needs. It was a 2BHK house that she had got on an economic rent because of its secluded location. She had turned one section of the hall into her office by separating it with the wooden divider, and the remaining area was used as a workshop. Out of the two rooms, she used one as a warehouse and the other she kept for herself, using it whenever she needed to be alone. Her staff used the kitchen for their morning and evening tea and snacks.

Recently, she had gotten an order of five paintings for an office that she needed to deliver in a fortnight. She grabbed her paintbrushes and pivoted toward the canvas. Painting was something that made her forget her past. With every stroke of the brush, she felt like she was better able to fight the demons buried deep inside her. Only she knew that behind the facade she wore for the world, there was an ugly side of her that she hated to look at. It's always easy to fight an enemy that is in front of you, but what if the enemy resides within you? In that case, you have already lost half the battle and winning the other half becomes next to impossible. So she did the next best thing and buried the enemy deep inside her while letting it eat away and make her hollow. She hardly let her tears fall, but she did let her heart bleed. While her brush smeared over the white base of the canvas, her heart felt the solace that she had been craving for. She had assumed that drowning herself in work and denying herself any pleasure would help soothe the pain of remorse. And by punishing herself this way, she would perhaps be able to forgive herself someday.

Engrossed in her thoughts and the colors, she lost all track of time. At five-thirty in the evening, her phone buzzed. It was her mother.

"Reeva, when are you coming back? Listen, I have called Shikha. She is good at makeup and hair styling," she heard her mother say breathlessly. She could also hear the bustling behind her. She could picture her mother busy in the kitchen, preparing all her expert dishes to please that super-rich suitor. What was his name? *Agnivesh Solanki*. There was a hue of distinctiveness to his name that had intrigued her first, but when she contemplated over it, she realized that they were no match for each other. She didn't even bother looking him up on Google or stalking him on social networking sites because somewhere she knew that this relationship wasn't going to happen. Sooner or later, he would realize that they weren't made for each other. Equality is must for any relationship to flourish, and they were at opposite ends in every way.

"Why did you call her, Maa? This isn't required; you know that I don't like makeup and all," she replied, exasperated. Shikha was her cousin and two years younger to her. She was popular in their group of cousins for her taste in fashion.

"Don't argue on this, and please, I beg you, listen to me for just today. Let everything happen according to me."

"Okay. I'll be back in half an hour."

"You better be quick. Agnivesh will be here around seven," said her mother. Reeva noticed the jitter in her mother's tone as she took Agnivesh's name, and it fueled her doubts even more. She terminated the call and turned her phone to silent mode before resuming her painting.

It was six-thirty when she left her workshop and headed home. Numerous missed calls flashed on her phone's screen as soon as she woke it up. She called back on her mother's number to assure her that she would be back in ten minutes.

Once she reached home, her mother ushered her into the bedroom and told Shikha to get her ready. Hours flew by, but there was no sign of Agnivesh. Her father called on his personal assistant's number, but it went straight to voice mail. Manish Rai, personal assistant to Agnivesh Solanki, was the one who had brought this proposal for Reeva in the first place. She was surprised at how effortlessly he had been able to convince her parents for this proposal, despite the fact that they knew nothing about Agnivesh then.

The buzz on her father's phone caught everyone's attention. It was Manish's call and he informed her father that they were on their way. Relief cascaded over her parents' faces, whereas Reeva remained indifferent. She had stopped expecting anything from life long ago. There was nothing that could affect her more than what she had already gone through before. There is a threshold to bearing pain too. Once you have touched that line, nothing affects you as much as it did before.

As soon as the doorbell rang, Prakash and Sumitra rushed to the door to welcome the guests. Two men entered the house with a large gift pack of dry fruits and sweets and four square-shaped red velvet boxes that seemed to hold jewelery. The next person to enter the house was Manish. They kept looking at the door fervently, expecting Agnivesh to join them next, but when no one followed, Prakash threw a questioning glance at Manish. He cleared his throat in response and signaled the man who stood next to him to open the boxes. The man followed Manish's command and started opening the boxes. As he opened the first box, Prakash asked him to stop and looked at Manish dubiously.

"What is this? Where is Agnivesh?" he asked directly.

"There was an urgent meeting in Mumbai, so Mr. Solanki had to leave for the same. But he has sent all these gifts and sent me to apologize on his behalf."

Silence took over the place. Sumitra and Prakash looked at each other. Prakash had smelled something suspicious in this whole scenario a long time back, but Sumitra had brainwashed him. He had ignored everything, despite Reeva's warnings. Sumitra smiled at Prakash, then turned towards Manish.

"We can understand, he is a busy man and has to manage everything single-handedly," she said.

"Yes, very true. Sir has instructed me to fix this alliance. It's a 'yes' from his side," said Manish, smiling.

Her mother beamed with happiness, but her father remained silent. After pondering for a moment, he said in a stern voice, "But it's a *'no'* from our side."

As soon as the words escaped his mouth, Sumitra gasped and Manish shifted on his feet uncomfortably.

"Sorry, Mr. Rai, but my daughter is not a burden on my shoulders and her happiness means the world to me. All these things that you have brought with you don't ensure her happiness. For me, she is much more valuable than these diamonds."

Her mother tried to intervene, but he stopped her by holding his hand up.

"She doesn't need these materialistic things. She needs a life partner. And all these things"—he gestured towards the gifts perched on the table—"are like a slap on our face. If he can't respect her, he doesn't deserve her. End of story." He glanced at Manish. "Please take all these things back along with those bangles that you brought earlier."

Manish tried to say something, but Prakash's fierce stare stopped him from doing it. Prakash silently motioned Sumitra to bring the bangles and then gestured the men to pick up the boxes and leave. Reeva ambled toward her father and hugged him.

"I am so proud to be your daughter, Daddy. I love you," she whispered.

"Always," said Prakash, caressing her back.

***

# All About Sona

**6 January, 2012**

*Dear Diary,*

*Are you surprised?*

*Why am I writing to you all of a sudden, when I have never done anything like this before? Something happened today, and for the first time in so many years, I am eager to share it with someone. Who can be more reliable than you? Moreover, no one has the patience to listen to my talks, because whenever I open my mouth to speak, everything gets tangled up. Yes, my speech is impaired, I stutter, and this is another reason why I am writing all this. But let's not talk about me here, let's talk about 'her'.*

*Surprised again?*

*Yes, it's a girl. A girl I saw at my college today. And after seeing her, the first word that came to my mind was 'Sona'. It's not her real name, but I am going to call her by this name. It's not the girlfriend kind of Sona, but real gold. She glowed with the blaze of a sunrise, just like gold. She looked pure, yet fierce, just like gold. So I named her 'Sona'. She wore a worn out jeans with a yellow collar-neck tee, and her short hair bounced up and down with her steps. Her face was red and her nostrils flared with fury. There was nothing angelic about her, and especially in this avatar of hers, she looked like a lady hooligan, yet I started adoring her the moment I first saw her. She is petite and lean, but still, in her anger, she radiated the energy of a sumo wrestler. I loved her the very instant I saw her. Is this what they call love at first sight? She stormed straight into my class and headed towards the last bench where I was sitting.*

*'Was all the rage that she oozed for me?' A thought popped up instantly, and I wouldn't have been surprised if it was true. Sometimes, I feel that half the people I know (or*

*don't know, for that matter) are angry with me. She broke my trance by grabbing the collar of the boy sitting next to me with her left hand and slapping his face with her other hand. Everything happened so instantly that it alarmed me. What if she hit me too? I don't hit girls back.*

*"How dare you? If I ever see you around her again, I swear to God, I'm going to kill you," she threatened him and was gone the very next instant, leaving me there imbued with her thoughts. I looked at the boy who was still trying to grasp what had just happened. One of his hands was still pressed against his cheek that had grown red because of the tight slap. He turned his gaze towards me and said, "I followed her friend...just once." He looked embarrassed. I looked at him with disgust too, not because of what he had done, but just because Sona hated him. This is what a single look from her had done to me. Since then, I have been unable to efface her image from my mind. So I thought, maybe writing will help.*

*Other people have friends to share their first crushes with, but I don't have any because I am incapable of holding that sort of an arrangement. I have already fucked up all my previous relationships. The last college I attended expelled me on the second day itself because I smashed a boy's head against the wall. He was bullying me. He made fun of the way I speak. I can't stand it when someone bullies me. I know, people here think that I am a psycho. Some call me a lunatic, while some call me belligerent. I am only a young nineteen-year-old boy with a height of six feet and two inches and a muscular build, but no one sees that. They all only notice my broken speech. Just because I stammer and can't tolerate someone making fun of my incapability, doesn't mean I am a lunatic.*

*I am possessive of my things too, and this obsession has gotten me into many troubles before. I remember the fight I had a few months ago when a group of boys scratched my Porsche. I was again on the verge of expulsion, but my father has always been on my side, despite being very strict with me at home. When he came to know about this incident, he bought a significant share of this college, so that no one could expel me ever. In return, I had to promise my father that I wouldn't talk to anyone here and would not indulge in any trouble. But now, I feel like breaking my promise because I so want to know more about Sona. She seems just like me... fierce and dangerous.*

*What would it be like to be her friend?*

*How would it feel to sit next to her?*

*What would it be like to listen to her talk?*

*All these thoughts are making my stomach flutter and are causing goosebumps to rise on my skin. This feeling is so novel and unfamiliar to me. I am going to end it here, as I am yet to know her. I will come back to you, Diary, when I see her next. And I am determined to see her again.*

~

# 2

Prakash and Sumitra, Reeva's parents, felt entirely thwarted by the happenings of the previous day. They hadn't expected that a marriage proposal from a magnate like Agnivesh Solanki would turn out to be such a joke. It was already three-thirty in the morning, but sleep was far away from their eyes.

"What does he think of himself? How dare he think so lowly of us? That bastard thinks he can buy my daughter with his diamonds," Prakash muttered under his breath.

"Calm down. Maybe it was urgent, that's why he had to leave in such a haste and didn't get time to inform us," Sumitra tried to soothe him.

"Stop defending him. Whatever it is…it's over now. Let's not talk about this anymore," Prakash said, a vein throbbing on his forehead. He leaned back against the headboard of their bed. He felt worried about his daughter. He knew that something was wrong with her. Reeva hadn't taken her grandfather's death well and that incident had changed her entirely. She wasn't the same girl she had been four years back. Though she tried to hide everything under her smile with utter perfection, the reality was that even that smile wasn't the same.

A sudden scream from Reeva's room made them bolt upright. They rushed to her room and found her squirming in bed, as if trying to fight someone. She was covered in sweat, looking frightened and trapped. Sumitra had to shake her awake. Reeva shot up straight in bed, gasping for breath and completely disoriented. It took her a while to realize where she was. Sumitra took her face in her hands and Reeva instantly wrapped her arms around her. Her heart was pounding so fast that she felt it might explode any moment.

"Are you okay, Reeva?" Sumitra asked, but didn't get any reply from Reeva. She didn't prod further. This wasn't new; Reeva had these kind of nightmares every other night. Despite her parents' repeated insistence, she never agreed to consult a doctor. For the sake of their satisfaction though, Reeva had endorsed the idea of visiting astrologers and did everything they told her to do. She never considered consulting a counselor. Why would she have gone to a counselor anyway when she knew very well what was troubling her! You can hide your demons inside you and fool the world that everything is all right, but how will you trick your own conscience? Reeva was still shaking with fear as those dreadful images haunted her mind.

"Are you okay, *beta*?" her father asked, caressing her back.

Reeva closed her eyes and gathered herself. She then quickly disengaged herself from her mother and smoothed back her hair.

"It was just a dream, a terrible one," Reeva said and then laughed grimly before adding, "I am fine. Sorry to disturb you."

"Stop pretending, Reeva." Her mother glared at her, riled up. "We all know very well that everything is not fine. And these aren't just bad dreams; they seem more like fits of panic."

"You don't have to hide your problems from us, Reeva. We love you and are always here to help you," her father said. Reeva looked at him, then turned her gaze to her mother. The concern and pain on their faces pierced through Reeva's chest, but instead of replying, she started laughing. Her parents looked at each other worriedly.

"Oh God! Please stop being so dramatic. Both of you"—she waved her finger, gesturing at her parents—"are searching for an imaginary problem that doesn't even exist. You guys just need something to worry about, don't you?" Reeva said, getting up from her bed and heading towards the washroom. Once inside, she let all the bridled emotions that she was concealing from her parents fall from her eyes in the form of tears. Over the past few years, Reeva had made herself strong enough, but these nightmares always penetrated through the shield she had built around herself and never let her forget that day. Turning the tap, she cupped her hands underneath to fill it with water and splashed her face thrice with it.

When she came out of the washroom, she saw her parents still sitting there on her bed. "Oh God! You are still here? Please go and sleep," she scolded, dabbing her face with a towel. Both of them glanced at each other, then left her room. Once they were out, Reeva slid back inside her blanket and made a futile attempt to sleep. She kept tossing and turning in bed till dawn drew closer and the sun devoured the darkness.

Hours passed and she got occupied with the hustle and bustle of the next day. Back at her workshop, she got busy checking the packaging of handmade clutches that were needed to be delivered that day. The order was for a baby-shower ceremony, where the hosts were going to present these as return gifts to their guests.

"Radhika, I hope you have checked the quality of all these clutches," Reeva asked one of her team members.

"Don't worry. We all know how particular you are about the quality!" Radhika replied.

"Have you prepared the quilt for the baby?" she quirked a brow at her.

"Yes, have a look," Radhika said and unfolded a small quilt in front of her. Reeva glanced at the square-shaped baby quilt made out of blue and pink silk cloth.

"It's perfect. Good job, Radhika," she smiled at Radhika who beamed at the compliment. It was an unspoken rule at *Kreative Krafts* that if the order were for some providential occasion, they would give a complementary gift along with the merchandise. Once she had checked through all the two hundred clutches, she packed them all again in a carton and called the delivery boy to take them away. She felt exhausted, but still turned to her canvas to complete the painting. In the time she finished the portrait, it was already dark outside and everyone else had left the workshop. She locked the workshop and headed towards the main road. She used to walk home most days, but felt too tired that evening, so she waved for an Auto and slid in.

As she climbed out of the Auto, the sight of a black Porsche parked outside her apartment made her halt in her tracks. She glanced at the car wistfully. It was *his* favorite car. She remembered how possessive *he* had been for his car. She brushed her hand slowly over its surface as if ruminating on some memories. As she reached near the driver's window, she ducked to look inside. Two dark and big eyes glared back at her, instantly scaring her out of her wits. She immediately backed off, her hand resting over her pounding heart. Was she expecting *him* inside the car? She shook her head at the thought.

Reeva rang the doorbell of her apartment and her mother opened the door almost instantly. As she entered, she noticed someone sitting in the living room, but before she could have a proper look at the guest, her mother quickly ushered her into her bedroom and latched the door behind them.

"Who is there?" Reeva asked her mother, frowning at her frantic activities.

"Agnivesh," Sumitra smiled, then added, "And if you thought earlier that he looked good in the photograph, it is nothing compared to seeing him face to face. He is damn gorgeous!"

"What is he doing here?" Reeva asked, rolling her eyes at her mother's exaggerated description.

"He is here to apologize for his behavior yesterday. He is a good guy," said Sumitra, rummaging through Reeva's almirah.

"Good guy! To hell with him," Reeva muttered under her breath.

"Now get up and wear this saree," Sumitra said, taking out the same saree that Reeva had worn the previous day.

"Oh, please! I am not going to doll up all over again. You know I hate it."

"Okay then, at least change out of these clothes and wear something decent."

"Decent? What is the problem with this attire?" Reeva gestured to the jeans and white top that she had on.

"Everything! Just look at yourself in the mirror once," Sumitra said, pointing at the spots of paint on her top.

"Whatever. It was your day yesterday. I did everything as you told me to. But today, it's my day," she said irately.

"At least comb your hair," her mother pleaded, joining her hands to her.

Reeva turned towards the dressing table exasperatedly and started combing her hair. "I am telling you now, it's not going to work. This relationship is already moot," she muttered.

Her mother sighed and threw her hands up in the air. "Do whatever you want to do. It's irrational to have any discussion with this girl," she said and left the room.

Soon after, Reeva entered the living room. Her mother smiled looking at her as she had changed into a blue printed Anarkali suit and had minimally applied make-up too. Though she had pleated her hair in a braid, a few silky strands hung loose and framed her round face perfectly, making her look even more adorable. "Only for you," Reeva mouthed at her mother, and she nodded in response.

Reeva glanced at the back of the guy sitting on the sofa. His broad masculine shoulders were in a well-defined shape. As she drew closer, her knees wobbled and she suddenly felt frail and mediocre. This man was indeed an epitome of beauty and grace. Dressed in a grey shirt with black tailored pants, he radiated an aura of power, confidence and perhaps arrogance too. Reeva noticed that he didn't glance at her when she stood beside the sofa he was sitting on, even though he had sensed her presence there, made evident by his gestures.

Had she ever seen this man before? Reeva tried to recall.

No, she hadn't ever met this man in her life. His personality wasn't something one could forget easily. Why was this man so fervent to marry her? Various questions started bugging her mind. She kept all her perturbations aside and marched past the sofa to stand in front of him and extended her hand.

"Hi, I am Reeva Panchal," she said, switching to the voice she usually reserved for her business meetings.

He stood up, and she noticed he was around a foot taller than her. He held her hand firmly to shake, and Reeva instantly felt a jolt at his touch.

"Hi, I am Agnivesh." His voice was commanding and intimidating which made Reeva lose her confidence for a moment. She cleared her throat and took the seat adjacent to him. She took her time to study his appearance and make her own judgments about him. He appeared like he would take no nonsense from anyone, so she decided to talk forthrightly without sugarcoating her words. She started to open her mouth to speak but stopped upon seeing her mother glaring at her and gesticulating to keep quiet.

Not bothering to stick to the sick norms of society, where a girl is expected to sit quietly and reply to questions in only a yes or no, she made up her mind to express the doubts that had been hovering in her mind for a long time.

"Before we take this meeting forward, I have some queries," Reeva said, and her voice sounded rude, even to her own ears. All the three pairs of eyes snapped in her direction immediately.

"Yes. I am all ears," Agnivesh said, pursing his lips. His voice was calm, but the shift in his demeanor told Reeva that he might have been a bit offended by her straightforwardness. But she didn't care.

"How did you come to know about me?"

He glanced at her with an unreadable expression on his face, then smirked with a flicker of inquisitiveness in his eyes.

"I visited your profile on a matrimonial site. I liked it and approached you," Agnivesh answered, locking his eyes with hers. Reeva looked back at him dumbfounded with her brow furrowed in confusion. She then turned her gaze towards her parents.

"Do I have a matrimonial profile?" she asked her father, surprised.

"Umm...we were about to tell you about that," her father replied. Reeva shook her head in disbelief and sighed. She returned her gaze to Agnivesh and studied him considerately. There was nothing odd in approaching someone through match-making websites. Hmm...but why her? Another question poked her mind.

"You can get any girl. Any girl who has the same status as you, then why me?" She dared to look into his eyes and return his stare.

"Maybe I found something in you that I have been unable to find in any other girl," Agnivesh replied and Reeva saw his eyes gleaming with an intense light. Her father's chest swelled with pride. This man had never undermined the worth of his daughter; he knew that she deserved all the happiness in the world. According to him she deserved Agnivesh more than he deserved her.

"And regarding the status, if having a healthy bank balance is what you call status, then I don't need it. For me, status is a desire, a passion and a fire, which is palpable in your eyes. And looking into them, I can say that we are equal in status. I want someone who understands that my business will always be my first priority," Agnivesh completed, still searching for something in her eyes. Reeva found herself hog-tied under his gaze. This wasn't the answer she had expected. Yes, she was passionate, desirous and way too devoted when it came to her dreams, but how could he have known all this by only looking into her eyes?

"If so, then what about all that diamond jewelery? What were you trying to prove?" The agitation in Reeva's voice was evident. He didn't reply for a moment, but simply kept looking at her.

"I wasn't trying to prove anything, Ms. Panchal. It's just that I have no elder to guide me in this regard, so I approached you the way I felt appropriate. I am sorry if it offended you." His voice was calm but firm. With his eyes still locked with Reeva's, Agnivesh stood up.

"I need to leave now. I have a flight back to Mumbai in next an hour. I would be grateful if I could get your response before leaving," he said.

"Umm…I…I need some time to think," Reeva stuttered, and Agnivesh nodded. The disappointment was etched clear on his face and it didn't go unnoticed by Reeva.

"Okay then," Agnivesh turned to Reeva's parents and held his hand out to her father. "It was nice meeting you, Mr. Panchal." He nodded at her mother and turned to leave.

"Reeva will escort you down," Reeva's mother spurted out, while Reeva glared at her.

Agnivesh looked at Reeva. "Of course," Reeva smiled squeamishly at him.

They both climbed down the stairs and walked towards the main road in an awkward silence. There was so much to say, yet nothing could be formed into words. That silence felt so earsplitting that all other voices around Reeva became insignificant. She didn't notice the bump in the road ahead and tripped over it. She would have stumbled headlong onto the road had Agnivesh not pulled her back just in time. The tight hold of Agnivesh against his chest with his arm wrapped around her made Reeva very conscious of his proximity. His pleasant fragrance swamped her senses, and suddenly she felt utterly entranced by the feeling of him so close to her. His eyes were dark and mysterious, just like the ocean at night, and his lustrous tousled black hair complementing his defined and graceful face. She felt sheltered in the refuge of his firm and masculine arms.

"Are you okay?" Agnivesh asked, and Reeva couldn't help but notice his dark brows furrowed in concern. She nodded, losing herself under the gaze of the man who was still a mystery to her. He loosened his grip around her and moved his other hand up to cup her face. Reeva surprised herself by leaning into his touch. The caress of his hand felt warm to her as if she was well acquainted with this touch. Her eyes were still locked with his, as if they both were in a bubble, away from the rest of the world.

"Please, say *yes*." The rasping voice of Agnivesh felt like music to her ears, as if it was the only voice present there. She found herself nodding again, entirely under the spell of the man who had meant nothing to her just a moment ago; the man she had been trying to run away from; the man who was the most unsuitable groom for her. Had she said '*yes*' to the marriage proposal? She most certainly did. The sides of Agnivesh's lips quirked up in triumph which made Reeva realize that she was giving in too quickly. She straightened herself on her feet and cleared her throat.

"I mean, I will think about it," she corrected herself instantly.

Agnivesh frowned skeptically and said, "I will wait for your response."

They started moving towards the main gate again, leaving behind the silence that had haunted them a moment ago.

"You have your main office in Mumbai, right?" asked Reeva, glancing furtively at the man she was walking with, too cautious to lose herself to him again.

"Yes. I work there, though I often have to come back here to look after my father's textile business," Agnivesh said in his smooth yet commanding voice.

"Oh," Reeva said. There was a hint of disappointment in that one word. She had given her blood and sweat to raise her business to the level it was at now. Though it wasn't as big as Agnivesh's, it was her everything nevertheless. If she said yes, she would have to move to Mumbai with him, leaving her dream behind. Was she considering his proposal? She didn't even realize that she was rubbing the knuckles of her hands, a habit of hers when she was confused or anxious.

"You won't have to give up your business," said Agnivesh, as if reading the dilemma in her gestures. She beheld his gaze, her brows rutted in confusion.

"I am planning to move back here permanently," Agnivesh said, poring over the confusion engraved on her face. Reeva let out a breath that she had been holding unintentionally. They had reached the main gate now. It was time to say goodbye. Reeva interlaced her fingers together, unable to decide whether to shake hands or if just a wave would be enough. She stiffened at the sudden touch of his hand on her back. He pulled her slightly towards himself and planted a kiss on her forehead.

"I will call you tomorrow," he whispered against her forehead, sending a jolt through her body. She froze, unable to comprehend what had just happened. She saw him walking away from her. His driver opened the back door of the car and he slid gracefully in. Her eyes widened in surprise when she noticed the car. The black Porsche. The same car that had reminded her of *him* only a few moments ago.

*His favorite car.*

***

# All About Sona

**4 February, 2012**

*Dear Diary,*

*You know what, it's been almost a month today, and I am yet to see Sona. But it feels like I am meeting and talking to her everyday in my thoughts. Since that little encounter with her, she has kindled hope in me. I am eager to be close to her and get to know her more. I am dreaming of my future with her. And it looks so perfect.*

*Is that impossible? A future with her?*

*Perhaps no, but I know how my fate plays games with me. Life has always been unfair to me. I feel my life is my biggest enemy. Always eager to snatch whatever happiness I have. How can I forget that dreadful accident I was in, six years back? My best friend, Roney, and I were coming back from a birthday party when our car met with a head-on collision. It was a near-death experience for me. Roney, my best friend, and my driver died in front of my eyes. I was just thirteen then. I lost my only friend at that tender age. With him, I also lost a part of myself, the part that was always fervent to make new friends.*

*My sole happiness was in my ability to conquer any debate. At the age of twelve, I won the National Debate Championship, but my life loves bitching me out. When I woke up after that incident, I learned that I had lost my voice. That was the end of the world for me. It took almost a year of rigorous treatment to regain my voice, but I couldn't complete a sentence in one go. I stammered, and I still do. A winner of almost every debate competition was unable to speak even a sentence without stammering. People around me started bullying me, and I started responding to their jibes by thrashing them. Soon, I grew completely belligerent.*

*To save other people and myself, I began distancing myself. I used to look at myself and wonder, why had God even kept me alive when I had nothing to look forward to in life?*

*But not anymore.*

*The moment I saw Sona, I knew the purpose of my life. She is my hope. But due to my terrible experiences before , I am no surer if I will get to see her again. How is it even possible that we are in the same college, yet I can't find her? I missed my classes. I even tried to go through every student's profile in my college. In short, I left no stone unturned, but no luck. And now, my hopes are diminishing with every passing moment. Shall I consider it another quip of life?*

~

# 3

Early morning the next day, Reeva woke up from a nightmare again, hot and bothered with a hammering heart. She thanked God for not having woken up her parents this time. Reeva had considered consulting a doctor many times, but then baulked at the idea. How could anyone have helped without seeing the demons that she had buried deep within her? There was no way she could reveal her secrets. She clambered out of the bed and marched towards the kitchen to get herself a cup of tea. She quietly took out a pan, careful not to disturb her parents sleeping in the adjacent room. She poured in some water and was about to keep the pan over the gas stove when a voice startled her, "Reeva?"

She turned to see her mother standing in the doorway.

"Oh! Did I disturb you? Go back to sleep. I just wanted a cup of tea," Reeva said.

"Did you wake up from a nightmare again?"

Reeva paused for a moment at her mother's question, then regained her composure and replied, "No! I am not sleepy actually."

"Mmhm," her mother said. "What did you decide about Agnivesh?"

"Umm...I am still thinking," Reeva replied, and her mother threw her hands up in disappointment.

"What is there to think so much? He is the best for you. I am telling you," her mother coaxed.

"Do we have to talk about this early in the morning?" she asked, resuming the task at hand.

"Let her decide in her own time. Don't push her, Sumitra." Both the ladies spun on their heels to find Prakash standing in the doorway.

"Look who is talking! The one who couldn't take a single correct decision in his life himself," Sumitra said heatedly.

"Stop it, Sumitra," Prakash warned. "This is about Reeva's life, and I won't let you snatch her right to choose—"

Sumitra cut him off holding her hand up. "Enough! Her right of decision? Seriously? Just look at her"—she waved her hand up and down, gesturing at Reeva—"This is what she has done with her life."

Her words stung deep in Reeva's heart. She instantly started fidgeting with the gas lighter to hide her anxiety. Her parents kept fighting, while she closed her eyes in introspection. *Were her desires, her beliefs, and her self-respect more important than her parents? Couldn't she sacrifice a little of her dignity for the sake of her parents' happiness? They had already gone through a lot because of her. She had shattered their dreams. If a 'yes' from her could give them joy, then why not?*

"I will marry him," Reeva's loud voice rent the air and made her parents jolt on the pitch. "If that's what makes you happy, I will do it for you. But please, stop fighting." Her voice was more calm and composed this time. She assured her father with a nod and left the kitchen without the tea.

Later through the day, she busied herself at the workshop, preparing for a meeting with the Royal Exposition Mart

(REM) Ltd. who had considered her handmade products for an expo at a niche aristocratically built hotel. A vibration on her phone caught her attention. She was getting a call from a landline number with a code she couldn't recognize, so she decided to turn a deaf ear.

"Do you know which city does the code 022 belong to?" Reeva asked Radhika after her phone had rung for the third time, flashing the same number. "Someone's calling me again and again," she added without looking at her, engrossed in the documents she had prepared for the meeting.

Radhika looked up, still holding the piece of jewelery she was adorning with pearls. She pursed her lips as if trying to recall. "Umm...I think it's Mumbai," Radhika said, "Yes! It's Mumbai."

The mention of Mumbai brought Reeva to a standstill. Could this be Agnivesh's call? Why would he call her from a landline number? Her phone buzzed again, dragging her out of her trance. She quickly hit the flickering green sign on her phone.

"Hello," she said.

"Hello, am I talking to Ms. Reeva Panchal?" A saccharine and a crisp female voice addressed from the other end. Reeva felt disappointed realizing it wasn't from him.

"Yes," said Reeva after clearing her throat.

"Good morning, Ma'am, it's Menasha from Agni Group of Hotels. This call is to fix an appointment with you regarding a telephonic conversation with Mr. Solanki. Is 4:35 PM today good for you?" Menasha asked and waited for Reeva's response.

Reeva felt perplexed at her words. This wasn't a business meeting that required a formal appointment. He could have called directly on her phone, but no. How could he? After all, he had to show her how busy he was! Reeva clenched her handset tight in her hand to appease her senses. '*Okay, if he wants to play it like this, then I am going to answer him in his tone*,' she whispered to herself.

"Sorry, I won't be available at that time." Reeva twisted her wrist to check the time and then added, "How about 11:30 AM today?" She had purposely chosen this time, a peak office hour.

"I am so sorry, ma'am. Mr. Solanki's schedule is entirely occupied between 10 and 4. Anytime between 4:20 to 4:50 will be fine for him."

Reeva stifled a chuckle at the response, then replied, "Drop it then, we can do it some other time because I am occupied for the rest of the day." She terminated the call without waiting for a response from the other side. Though it was insignificant, she rejoiced at this small triumph.

Soon after securing all the required documents in a file, she left for the meeting. It was one of the most supreme expos in Surat where many entrepreneurs got a chance to manifest their handiwork to the elite of the city. Getting this deal was crucial for her. Though she had reached thousands of people through e-commerce, she was yet to establish a strong offline presence, and this was the chance for her.

She reached the venue and glanced at her wristwatch; it was five past eleven in the morning. Though she was late by five minutes as per the reporting schedule, she was asked to wait for a few more minutes, not that she had any complaints with that. Her phone buzzed in her bag. She decided to ignore it first, but then took it out to check who was calling. It was an unknown number. She took the call, just in case it was from one of her customers.

"Hello," Reeva said, holding the mobile precariously between her shoulder and ear. The voice from the other end sent a chill down her spine. Though Reeva wasn't acquainted with him all that well, she recognized Agnivesh's voice instantly. She checked the time. It was 11:30 A.M. dot. She was still battling her bewilderment when the receptionist called her name out for the meeting.

"Umm…er…hi," she stuttered, struggling to come up with an appropriate response. She closed her eyes momentarily and inhaled a deep breath. "I am busy right now, and it's really important for me. I'll talk to you later," she said and disconnected the line without waiting for his response.

The meeting went fine; the organizers liked her presentation and appreciated her products. but the biggest challenge was arranging funds. Though they agreed to take the amount in instalments, but with all the other bills, it was difficult for her to arrange that monthly payment even. It was a big opportunity for *Kreative Krafts* and she didn't want to miss it, so she decided to apply for a loan. She felt so disoriented after the meeting that she completely forgot to call Agnivesh back. But when she remembered, she decided to apologize. She pulled out her phone only to find a text from him that read: **The first rule of business is to value time, not just your own but others' too. There was a reason why I called to fix an appointment.**

Reading the text, she felt humiliated. Her cheeks grew red in embarrassment. She was undoubtedly wrong here, so she typed a message back: **I am extremely sorry. 4:35 PM is fine for me.**

She returned back to her workshop and got involved in an ongoing consignment. The day passed in the blink of an eye. She often checked for Agnivesh's response in between, but didn't receive any. Sharp at 4:35 PM, her phone buzzed again. It was a message from Agnivesh.

**Have dinner with me. Tomorrow at Leonardo. My driver will be there at your apartment by 6 PM.**

She rolled her eyes at the message and bit back a smile. Damn! The man sounded intimidating even on text. She considered joining him for dinner. She had an urge to refuse the drive, but then decided against it. She owed him that at least after her unprofessional behavior. Unprofessional? Really? They weren't in this colloquy for business, yet he treated it like a business deal. She was mature enough, however, to understand that everyone had their own way of handling things and that one should respect the other's individuality. The one thing that Reeva had learnt from her experience was — you can't really change people, so learn to accept them as they are. And if you can't accept them, it's better to let them go, because they aren't meant for you.

***

# All About Sona

**29 March 2012**

*Dear Diary,*

*Mark this day. Today, after one month, twenty-four days and eighteen hours, I saw her again. Yes, I saw Sona. I seldom go to the sports complex at college, but my destiny took me there today. I had to submit my assignment to our professor of Economics. Don't you find it strange? Why would a professor summon his student, who couldn't submit his assignment on time, to the sports complex, that too after college hours? But it happened just so, and I can't thank my stars enough that it happened. After submitting the assignment, I was passing by the badminton court when I saw her. Suddenly, everything seemed to happen in slow motion; she was playing badminton, her T-shirt was drenched in sweat and clung to her body. She played with the same bounce in her feet that I had seen earlier, but this time, she carried a smile on her face. I noticed that her hair had grown out a little since I saw her last. Though she had tied them up in a small ponytail, a few stubborn silky strands kept falling over her face, as if it was difficult for them to stay without caressing her face every few seconds. I don't blame them either, she is breathtakingly beautiful. She was incessantly tucking them behind her ears. Watching her game, the one thing I have learnt about her is that she isn't a very good player. Her racquet hardly hit the shuttlecock, yet she kept on trying. While she was busy playing, I went to check the entry register to know her credentials. There weren't many entries, just six boys and one girl. But I could see two girls on the field, she and her friend. Perhaps only one of them had made the entry which was by the name Gayatri, from Science department. I knew that it wasn't her name because life has never played easy on me. I will have to hunt some more to know about her. At least I have a clue now. I need to check student profiles from the Science Department. I closed the register and went back to the badminton court, but she wasn't there. She had left the place. I tried to look for her, but couldn't find her anywhere. I am happy nevertheless because I am hopeful now. Tomorrow, I will go to the sports complex again at the same time and then I will fill you with more details, diary. Till then, bye bye.*

~

# 4

"Are you going to wear this for dinner?" Reeva's mother asked, examining her top to down. She was wearing traditional Indian formals–a yellow cotton *salwar-kameez* with a plain folded cotton dupatta hanging down her shoulder. Her hair were neatly tied in a ponytail.

"And no makeup?" she added, looking at Reeva's bare face. The attire appeared more appropriate for some formal meeting, certainly not for a date. But then, that was how Agnivesh had made her feel, and now she was playing by his rules.

"Yes," she answered, "And trust me, this is apt for this meeting."

"Reeva, Reeva, what has happened to your dressing sense? There was a time when you were the style icon among your cousins. And look now," her mother said, baffled.

Yes! There was a time when she was entirely a different girl. Her mother didn't know how an incident four years back had crushed Reeva into pieces, and how she had gathered those pieces and molded them to be this *new* Reeva. How could she have possibly known when Reeva never told anyone what happened. Each and every second of her life, she pretended as if nothing had changed and that she was the same girl. This time too, she forced a smile on her face and kissed her mother on her cheek.

"Oh Maa, I'll change if you want me to, but trust me, I am more comfortable in this dress. Moreover, the driver is already waiting outside. It wouldn't be nice to keep him waiting. What do you say?" she asked her mother.

"Now don't act smart and go. And please be nice to him," Reeva's mother said, making Reeva roll her eyes instantly.

"I'll definitely be nice to him if he'll be nice to me. But based on his previous antics, I can't promise anything," Reeva retorted and left the house. The car was parked at the main gate – the same black Porsche. She slid into the back seat and heaved a sigh of relief upon seeing the rear seat empty. Though she hadn't wanted Agnivesh to come pick her, since she wanted some alone time to prepare herself for the meeting, she anticipated a little that he might come. The driver pulled away from the curb. It took them around twenty minutes to arrive at their destination. She walked into the restaurant and started looking for him. Unable to find him, she headed towards the reception to enquire if there was a table booked in his name.

"Is there a reservation—" she started but a firm hand on her back interrupted her, shooting a jolt up her spine. She recognized the touch instantly. He wore an aura around him that shouted power and domination. She looked up at him. Dressed in a white shirt and black tailored pants, he looked the personification of exquisiteness and glamour. The meek voice in her head started soaring again, '*Why did he choose me?*' He glanced at her and caught her gaze. A sly smile touched his lips as if he had read her mind.

"Good evening, Mr. Solanki, we have reserved the table for you upstairs," said the hostess, escorting them upstairs. His hand was still burning a hole in Reeva's back as he directed her through the restaurant. She felt relieved as he removed his hand and gestured her to sit.

They took their seats across the table form each other. Reeva began to feel awkward, and started looking at the interiors to distract herself. The place was beautiful, designed exquisitely by Italian theme. The beautiful paintings, off-white furniture and the concealed golden light behind the artistically designed ceiling created an ambience of perfect comfort, intimacy and romance. *Romance?* Where had this thought popped up from all of a sudden? She shook her head to evade the unwanted contemplation.

"Don't you like this place?" asked Agnivesh, misreading her gestures.

"It's nothing like that," she cleared her throat before adding, "The place is just fine." Agnivesh nodded. The server came to take their orders. Reeva wasn't too familiar with the Italian menu, so Agnivesh offered to help her, which Reeva accepted shyly. After the server left, an awkward silence rammed back into the space between them.

"It's a beautiful place," Agnivesh broke the ice.

"Indeed it is! But I think we aren't here to discuss the exquisiteness of this place. Shall we come to the point?" Reeva said, lacing her voice with confidence.

Agnivesh scratched his chin with his thumb, while his brooding eyes studied her. "Point?" he asked, smirking.

She returned his smirk and said, "I don't know much about you, but the one thing I have learned about you is that you wouldn't give someone the time of your day if you aren't getting benefitted from it. What's your benefit in this alliance?"

"Patience!" he raised his voice just a little, but it had an intimidating effect on Reeva. "Patience," he repeated, but his voice was calmer this time. "It's the second rule of business." He pinned her with his gaze, a devilish grin shadowing his face.

She laughed humorlessly. "Is this what we are here to discuss today? Business?"

He bored his eyes into hers and leaned forward on the table.

"We are going to discuss our lives"—he pressed his lips to a thin line—"our lives together, Reeva."

He leaned back and folded his arms over his chest. "And I don't see how it is any different from business."

Reeva frowned. Was he actually juxtaposing life with business? She couldn't believe it.

"No one in this world will stay in a relationship if they aren't getting anything out of it. We decide to share our life with someone because we get some benefit out of that alliance. We are here to discuss the benefits that you will be getting out of this relationship." He studied her expressions for a moment, then continued, "And of course, I will be sharing my own interests as well." Agnivesh elucidated as if he could read into her expressions with utter perfection. He waited for Reeva's response, but when he didn't get any, he added further, "Isn't a relationship just like business? Sharing of resources? Trading benefits? Don't you agree?"

Reeva exhaled audibly and looked straight into his eyes, "Maybe I am not as experienced as you in business, but if you are asking my opinion on relationships, then *no*. I won't call it a 'trading benefits'." She took a moment to search for the right words, then resumed, "Trading isn't the right word to use in the context of any kind of bond. It makes it worthless and hollow. 'Sharing' is the word; sharing of emotions and happiness, one's beliefs, and even the blues. For me, it will never be an equation of materialistic benefit."

Agnivesh crossed his legs and looked down at his glass. He appeared to be in deep thought as he grazed his index finger over the rim of the glass. Reeva looked at him, trying to comprehend his next move.

"Your parents called this morning and told me that you are ready for this alliance. Is it true?" he asked, still looking at his glass. "I believe them, but I still need to hear it from you," he completed, and this time, he looked up at Reeva.

Reeva was flabbergasted. She hadn't anticipated these words from him, neither had she expected her parents to have called Agnivesh that soon. Reeva felt all too aware of Agnivesh's constant gaze that told her that he was waiting for her response. She nodded hesitantly in a *yes*. A winning smile made the sides of his lips quirk up slightly, and Reeva instantly cursed herself for having given him this satisfaction. He crossed his arms over the table and leaned forward slightly.

"Why did you agree, Reeva? Are you ready to share with me your so-called happiness and emotions and beliefs?" he asked, his voice icy and stern. His question caught her off guard. He had skillfully trapped her in her own words. She couldn't come up with an answer and looked at him dumbfounded.

"Let me help you with an answer. You agreed because you saw your benefits in this offer," Agnivesh said, holding his chin between his fingers and thumb. '*Offer*'–the word rang in Reeva's ears.

"Money will never be the base of any relationship for me," Reeva stuttered due to the rage building up inside her.

"Then why did you agree? What do you know about me, except for my name and affluence?" Agnivesh asked, cocking his head to one side.

His question hit her hard. What did she know about him indeed? For a brief moment, deep within her heart, Reeva believed that she had agreed to his proposal because of his affluence. Her cheeks grew a deeper shade of pink due to this mortification. Was he doing it intentionally? Did he want to see her humiliated? Her eyes started to prick with fury.

"You agreed because you saw a secure future for yourself and...your business," he continued. Each of his words felt like a dagger piercing through her chest. Was he wrong? Probably not. She, or her parents, knew nothing about him, yet had agreed to his proposal. This is the thing about truth, easy to say when it is about others, difficult to accept when it is about you, and it does hurt more than a lie. But was it the truth? Had she said 'yes' just to secure her future?

No. She had agreed because of her parents, for the sake of their happiness. But her parents' illusory happiness wasn't more important than her dignity. Her blood boiled with fury. She knew that if she stayed there for another second, the wrath inside would burst out of her. She closed her eyes for a moment and stood up.

"This meeting is over," she declared. Agnivesh frowned, but the lines on his forehead disappeared soon. If he was hiding his disbelief, he was definitely good at it. She lifted her handbag from the table and adjusted its strap over her shoulder with shaky hands. She looked at him and found him staring at her unfathomably.

"And let me remind you, it was you who came to my door asking"—she shook her head and corrected herself—"sorry, begging for my hand. It wasn't..." She felt too choked to spurt out another word. " ...you know what, go to hell."

She spun on her heel and started to leave, but then stopped suddenly, looked over her shoulder and said, "And one more thing, it's a *no,* a big *no*," and walked out.

They say, one should go with the flow, but she was the one to always challenge the flow.

She moved out of the restaurant, leaving Agnivesh behind; leaving everything behind that had stirred up her balance; leaving his words behind that had shattered her confidence, and leaving his hauteur behind that had threatened to kill her individuality.

***

# All About Sona

30 March, 2012

*Dear Diary,*

*I have two things to tell you about Sona today. Let me start from the beginning. After college, I was back at the sports complex, but unfortunately, there was no sign of Sona. I searched for her all around, but couldn't find her. I checked the entry register too and there were a few entries, but none of them was in the name of Gayatri or any other name I could relate to Sona's face. Despite all the rage she exuded on the first day I saw her, she is still wonderfully exquisite in her own way. She can't have a common name. It has to be unique, just like her. Disheartened, I came out of the complex and had taken only a few steps when I saw her. Sitting on a bike at the curb in front of the complex, she was tapping her foot anxiously on the footrest. She was wearing a pink T-shirt and black tights. Her eyes were fixed on the road, as if waiting for someone. Maybe, her friend.*

*Why didn't she go inside? Why was she waiting outside in the sweltering heat? I tried to find the answers, but then I saw something that helped me connect the dots and I didn't like the inference. A boy riding a bike arrived soon after and parked his bike just next to Sona's. She suddenly rose to her feet, as if his sudden appearance had affected her. The boy jumped off the bike, removed his helmet and hung it at the back of his motorcycle. As he raked his hand through his hair, Sona ogled at him with her lips parted and face flushed. Had she been waiting for him? I didn't like the thought and dismissed it. The guy rounded her while she kept on looking at him, all doe-eyed. I liked that the guy didn't make any attempt to talk to her and left without even giving her a second glance. She was interested in him; I could see that much in her eyes and it was painful for me. Why am I feeling like this? I don't even know her, yet I feel possessive about her.*

*Once the guy was inside the complex, she sighed as if she had been holding her breath. I made a mental note to dig out information about this guy and keep him away from her. After a few minutes, her friend Gayatri appeared along with another boy, and they all went into the complex. I stood there wondering who the other guy with them was? Why didn't she go in earlier? And again, it was her friend who made the entry by showing her student ID card. So the things that I am assuming here are: She has a crush on that guy, which I don't like at all, and the second that she is not from our college because she didn't have a student ID card, without which no one is allowed inside the complex. Does that mean she comes here to gawk at that guy? The thought is unsettling and has been roiling in my gut, making it excruciating to bear with. Whatever it may be, it's certainly not a good news for me. I will soon update with new information, diary. Till then, bye bye.*

~

# 5

When Reeva exited the restaurant, Agnivesh's driver was already waiting at the curb. Perhaps Agnivesh had instructed him to be there. As soon as the driver saw her approaching, he opened the back door for her. She strolled towards it, but instead of getting into the car, she took the auto parked just beside the car. When she reached home a half an hour later, she expected that her mother would be ready to bombard her with questions. So, as soon as her mother opened the door for her, she scampered off to her room. Her mother took the hint from her behavior that the meeting hadn't gone well, but she asked her still, "Is everything alright, Reeva?"

Reeva pulled out her phone to call Radhika and shoved the handbag on her bed. Her mother asked again, "What happened, Reeva?"

"Nothing"—she shook her head, dialing a number on her phone—"absolutely nothing." When the call did not connect, she tossed her phone on the bed too. She rifled through her wardrobe and took out her night suit. Holding it over her arm, she sprinted towards the washroom.

"What do you mean by *nothing*? Wasn't Agnivesh happy with you? Did he say something?" her mother asked apprehensively.

Her mother's concern irked Reeva. She stopped at the washroom door and looked back at her irately. "What he said doesn't matter. The only thing you should be concerned about is what did I say, and I said *no*."

"Are you mad? What do you—"

Reeva cut her mother off by holding her hand up, "This topic is closed now. We aren't discussing it anymore."

"Who are you to close the topic? We are your parents, and we have all the right to decide for your future. Tomorrow, you are going to apologize to Agnivesh," her mother ordered.

Reeva turned and looked at her mother in disbelief. "No way," she said, tossing the cloths onto the bed.

"Who do you think you are? *Haan?* Just tell me, who are you? Are you a princess or Miss World? Stop pulling this kind of an attitude, Reeva. This is going to do you more harm than good, I am telling you."

"Sumitra, let her take her own decisions," Prakash, Reeva's father, intervened. The loud voices had drawn him to Reeva's room.

"What decision? Can't you see how she is spoiling her life and ours too? She used to be such a good girl. Talk about anything, and she'd ace in it. Now look at her, it's hard to believe she is the same girl that she used to be a few years back. This business of hers has ruined her senses," her mother carped heatedly.

"Yes! I am not the same girl and will never be that girl again. And why do you even want that girl back? So that you may brag about her achievements in your so-called society? Just because my definition of success is different than yours, doesn't mean I am a failure. This business is my identity, and you have to accept that. Why can't you accept me how I am today? Do you think about me even once? Every day, every damn day, I fight to pretend that I am the same girl, just because I want to see you happy. But now, I am tired of these pretences. I am who I am," Reeva said and her eyes welled up with the tears she had been holding for long.

Her mother threw her hands up in capitulation, "Okay! You do whatever you want to do, but please"—she folded her hands—"agree to this proposal. You have no idea, Reeva, how difficult it is to get an eligible groom like Agnivesh. Everyone wants a well-educated girl and an affluent family. You think someone as good as Agnivesh, who is a postgraduate from one of the top business schools in India, will ever agree to marry a girl who is not even a graduate."

The words buzzed in Reeva's mind as if she was in an acoustic trap. Everything around her went mute suddenly. She noticed her father saying something to her mother angrily, but nothing registered in her mind. She sank down to her bed with a thud. These few words were just enough to shatter her confidence that she had built over all these years. *What kind of a world are we living in, where degrees matter over talent, money matters over hard work, and success matters over satisfaction.* Reeva's mind felt clogged with these thoughts. Her parents kept fighting, but all she could hear was '*a girl who is not even a graduate*'.

We need to feel safe. Not from the outer world but from our own self. We try to build an armor with all positive thoughts around us, yet some words have the power to pierce through it and make us feel empty. Suddenly, Reeva started to feel numb to life. Failed and miserable. This nothingness was killing her from the inside. She felt she had to run away from this place if she wanted to save herself. This was what she had always done – run from the predicament that threatened her peace of mind. On an impulse, she bolted upright and started packing her things in a small duffel bag. Reeva was already zipping her bag up when her mother noticed her.

"What are you doing?" her mother asked, astounded.

“Leaving,” Reeva replied and lifted up her bag.

“Why?”

“Because I need space. I won’t be able to comply with what you expect me to do. So, it is better if I stay away from it for some time. I will be back when I feel alright,” Reeva said and sprinted out of the house. Her parents kept staring at her back, but they didn’t stop her. It wasn’t new for them. Reeva often left home and stayed at her workshop for a day or two, and then came back.

Once Reeva was on the main road, she waved for an auto and left for her workshop. This day had been another ordeal altogether, but thankfully, it was about to get over. Once at her workshop, she would indulge in her work, a tactic that always worked for Reeva. Upon reaching the workshop, she hunted for the keys in her bag, but couldn’t find them. She then remembered that she had told Radhika to keep the keys with her since she had to leave early for her meeting with Agnivesh. She wondered if the day could get any worse and sat down on the pavement dejectedly. She started thinking about all possible options where she could go and spend the night? She ruled out her relatives and friends as they would needle her for reasons. She decided to either go to Radhika’s place or a hotel. She rummaged through her bag again for her phone, only to realize the next moment that she had thrown it on her bed while in the argument and never picked it back up. She held her head in her hands for a moment, then rose up. She picked up her bag and sauntered on an empty road aimlessly. It was already past ten in the night and getting a dependable ride at that time was difficult.

She had hardly covered half a kilometer when suddenly she sensed someone following her. She didn’t look back, but paced up her strides. She noticed a rise in the pace of steps behind her as well and that got her damn terrified. Hugging her duffel bag, she hurried on as if it would be able to save her from the anonymous threat. The steps behind her started getting louder and closer, and before she could scream, she heard a voice.

"Stop, Reeva. Running is not the solution."

Suddenly, she halted in her tracks. She knew this voice. After humiliating her at the restaurant, the man had the audacity to come after her! She started walking again, pacing faster still.

"I am not searching for a solution, dammit! I am running away from you. Just leave me alone," she yelled, striding away from him. Why had this man come into her life? She had somehow gathered her shattered life over these past years, and this man had stirred up everything in a moment. Resentment started building up inside her like a speeding freight train. He ran after her and caught her by the arm. Without thinking twice, Reeva slapped him so hard that she felt the burn sting her hand too. He looked at her dumbfounded. Without giving him a chance to speak, Reeva pushed him frantically, making him stumble a few steps back.

"Just go away. Go far away from my life. I don't want you. I know why you have come into my life and I will never let you affect me, even if I have to fight you for it," Reeva yelled.

"You want to fight me? Come on. Come and fight with me," Agnivesh said, flexing two of his fingers in invitation. Surprisingly, she took the challenge. She was mad at him, mad at her parents and above all, mad at herself. She threw her bag on the road and strode ahead to push him once again, but this time, he didn't budge. She shoved both her arms against his chest as forcefully as she could, and as she did it, she felt as if a heavy weight was being lifted off her chest. It was a relief. Suddenly, Agnivesh grabbed both of her arms and pinned them behind her back. She wriggled against his firm hold, but he was too powerful compared to her. She looked up at him in surprise, still squirming under his grip. She hadn't expected him to fight back, but the fact that he did made her feel even more empowered somehow. He locked his gaze with her, and she felt the grip of his hands on her wrists loosening a little. She took the opportunity and freed her hands, jerking them out of his hold and hitting his groin at the same time with her knee. He stumbled back and grimaced in pain.

She suddenly felt concerned about his well-being. She walked up to him and asked, "Are you okay?"

He caught her by her wrist again and pinned it against her back. With his free hand, he grabbed her other arm and pushed her back until she was trapped against the wall. Everything happened so fast that she couldn't do anything. He pinned her legs with his knees so that she couldn't attack him there again. She used all her energy to get out of his grip, but he was too strong for her. Soon, she gave up and helplessness started clouding her face. Agnivesh brought his mouth close to her and whispered against her lips, "I am sorry."

She tilted her head slightly away to get a clearer view of Agnivesh's expressions. She wanted to understand whether he really meant that or if it was another ruse.

"I am sorry for my behavior today, Reeva. I have my own experiences that colour my perception of relationships a certain way, but that doesn't justify my behavior. I can't foist my viewpoint on you."

He loosened his grip a little, but Reeva didn't push him away. She felt emotionally wrecked and started sobbing soon, resting her forehead against his chest. He released her hands and she supported herself by holding his arms.

"It's going to be okay," Agnivesh whispered in her ear soothingly to calm her down.

"I am tired of running. I am tired of having to fight with everyone. I am tired of fighting with my own self. I can't help myself anymore. I have ruined the lives of everyone around me. I will ruin yours too. You should be scared of me," she blubbered. She didn't even realize until the words had escaped her lips that she was giving him a part of herself by sharing her demons with him. She had never let herself break down emotionally in front of anyone. Why was she letting him in? Why did she find solace in his embrace? Agnivesh caressed her back and let her cry her heart out without prodding further.

"The next time you feel like running, run to me. The next time you feel like fighting, fight me. When you feel that you can't help yourself, just let me help you. Let me be a part of your life, Reeva. There is a good possibility that we both will ruin each other, but in some relationships, ruining is the only way to fix one another. And we won't know it until we try," Agnivesh whispered softly into her ear, caressing her back incessantly. Reeva started melting under the warmth of his words. A part of her wanted to trust him. She wanted to believe in his idea of fixing each other. And at that moment, she felt hopeful.

Agnivesh pulled back slightly and brushed his fingers over her tear-streaked cheeks.

"Go back home, Reeva. Your parents are worried," Agnivesh said.

"I can't. Not today, at least," Reeva replied, looking at him.

"Then come with me," he said, narrowing his eyes, as if urging her. She nodded. She didn't have any other place to go anyway. But wasn't that strange? She had run away from home because of Agnivesh, and now she was going with him.

Agnivesh grabbed her hand with a sense of entitlement and Reeva instantly looked at their joined hands. His touch was awkward yet soothing. They walked hand in hand till they reached where Agnivesh's car was parked. It was the same car, but there was no driver this time. He opened the passenger door for her, then rounded the car to take the driver's seat. Reeva noticed that he had changed into a grey tee and blue denims, while she was still in the same attire she had on for dinner. He turned on the ignition and revved up the engine, glancing at Reeva occasionally. He sensed her discomfort.

"Are you okay?" he asked to start the conversation.

"Yeah, where are we going?"

"Umm...the hotel I am staying at."

"You are staying in a hotel? What about your home?" she asked, surprised. He had his father's house here in Surat, yet he was staying in a hotel.

"I don't go back to my house, Reeva. It haunts me. Once I had a complete family there, but now it's completely desolate. I lost everything in a blink of an eye," he said dejectedly. She didn't prod further. She had learned from her father that Agnivesh's father had died of heart attack and that his mother passed away only a few days after his father's death.

"Is that one of your hotels?" she asked to divert his mind.

"No, Reeva. I don't own any hotels in Surat yet," he said, and she nodded.

They left the car with a valet upon reaching the hotel where Agnivesh was staying. As soon as they were out of the car, Agnivesh reclaimed Reeva's hand and strolled into the hotel's lobby. They boarded the elevator that took them to the twelfth floor. Agnivesh took out the keycard from his pocket and unlocked the door. It wasn't just a room, but a full-fledged apartment. The door led into a sitting area first. There was a dressing room to the right, and a small open kitchen beside that. Further down was a huge bedroom with a king size bed, classy furniture, elegantly designed interiors, with an attached washroom. Agnivesh started removing his tee, and Reeva averted her gaze instantly.

"Are we going to share this room?" she asked hesitantly. She knew the answer, yet the question escaped her mouth. He wouldn't have brought her there if they weren't going to share that space. Momentarily, Reeva felt uncomfortable and started rubbing the knuckles of her hands.

"Yes. We are going to share this room and this bed too." He gestured towards the bed with his eyes. She looked at him and he met her gaze. "You have to trust me, Reeva," he added.

Could she trust him? She had no reason to trust him, but did she have any reason to mistrust him? She had already trusted him when she agreed to come with him. She didn't argue further. "Yeah," she nodded.

They ordered for dinner soon after. Reeva hadn't realized how hungry she was until food was placed on the table. She looked furtively at Agnivesh who was eating his food silently. He was so comfortable in her presence. It was soothing and intimate. For the first time since they had met, she felt that there could be a possibility of them being together. He didn't seem distant and arrogant anymore. In his night pyjamas and a worn out T-shirt, he looked so satiated and relaxed that Reeva couldn't help gawking at him.

"Eat your food, Reeva," he said without looking up at her. Perhaps he had sensed her eyes on him, and she stifled the blush on her face by pursing her lips. She started nibbling instantly like a bird.

Later, when Agnivesh chose to sit on the couch and work on his laptop, she sat down on the carpet at the bottom of the bed, resting her back against the bed-side. She was still lost in her thoughts when she felt a bustle beside her. She looked up to see Agnivesh taking a seat next to her. He stretched his legs and then looked at Reeva.

"Call your parents, Reeva. They are worried," he said.

"How do you know?"

"I called at your number to apologize. Your father picked up the phone and told me that you had left the house. He sounded anxious," he said, looking back and forth into her eyes.

She shook her head in response. "I am not going to call them. Why can't they understand a simple thing that I am not what they want me to be? I am tired of living on their terms."

"You know, Reeva, I was just twenty-one when my father asked me to join his textile business. I was adamant to pursue MBA and start something of my own. He gave me two options, either to choose my family or my dreams, and I chose the latter. I never got to enter my own house after that. It was only after his death that I stepped across that threshold again. And I still regret leaving them," he said. The pain was palpable in his voice.

"I am so sorry to hear that." Concern was etched clear on Reeva's face. "But my story is entirely different. I am fighting for my dignity with every single fiber of my being. Why can't they accept me as I am? They are my own, and instead of supporting, they always pull me down," she said and her eyes glossed over with grief and hopelessness.

Agnivesh leaned his head back and stared at the ceiling. "It's always our own, Reeva. Always. The most loved ones. The most trusted ones. The ones we consider the center of our universe. They pull us down to make us feel lousy, and they do so because we let them. We empower them to hurt us, to destroy us, to make us miserable. It's always our fault," he said.

Reeva sensed that his focus was diverted, he was no longer talking in a general sense. He had started to open up about his own experiences. Strangely, she felt relieved that she wasn't the only one struggling with demons inside. At that moment, he looked totally unlike himself. He looked vulnerable, despondent and perhaps...broken. Just like her. Since the time they had met, she felt for the first time that they were equal. They were similar in some certain yet unknown ways. Looking at him, she had the urge to touch him, to calm him, to soothe his pain that seemed all too familiar to her. The words were still unsaid, yet she could feel them. Wasn't that the right way of interaction between two people who were planning to spend the rest of their lives together? It kindled hope in her heart; perhaps she could heal him, perhaps he could heal her, perhaps they weren't meant to ruin, but to fix one another.

***

# All About Sona

9 April, 2012

*Dear Diary,*

*It's been six days in a row—minus the weekend—since I started stalking her at the sports complex. She is definitely not from our college and Gayatri is her friend. And yes, I still haven't gotten lucky enough to know her name. The guy whom she was gawking at that day is none other than the captain of the badminton team of the college. Raunak Patel is his name. That also explains why she is so eager to learn badminton. The guy is already in a relationship, so he is no threat. But what should I do with this girl? When he is around, she looks at him as if nothing else exists. Not to mention, it hurts. Badly. I can't let her dwell in the thought of being with him when he is already off limits. And the other guy who was with Gayatri that day is her boyfriend. His name is Vikrant Taneja and he is the most intelligent guy at college, already placed and working for a tech. firm.*

*I watched her from a distance again today for the entire evening. She played badminton for a while, then went to sit in the library alone; it's her daily routine. In denim shorts and a white tee, she looked so young and innocent. Her hair were untied today, and they kept falling over her face as she leaned over the table to read a book. I so want to touch her hair, listen to her talk and feel her closeness; I so want to sit with her and talk to her, but she hardly noticed me. I don't consider the option of walking up to her and introducing myself because even if I try, I won't be able to talk to her without stuttering, and the thought that she may bully me for my speech, or even pity me, scares me to hell. I know what effect it would have on me if I see either of that on her face. The thing that bothers me the most is my temperament. I would never forgive myself if I ever hurt her, and considering my previous antics, I know that my behavior is unpredictable. I may hurt her no matter how much I don't want to. I lose all control over my actions, and that leaves me with nothing but remorse.*

*Every time I see her, I feel like some unknown force is pulling me towards her. Have I developed some feelings for her? These unnamed feelings are strong enough to make me forget myself and overwhelm me with this new emotion. Being a part of her world is no longer a desire; it's slowly becoming a necessity for me with every passing day. Though I am not with her, she is there in my mind all the time. Am I not already in a kind of a relationship with her? So, I have decided to stay away and love her from a distance, rather than approaching her and ruining everything. I am a demon, while she is an angel. We aren't meant to be together.*

~

# 6

"Reeva, Reeva, wake up!"

Her eyes flipped open at the mention of her name. She was covered in sweat, her heart was pounding in her chest and her heavy breathing filled the room. It didn't take her much time to realize that she had had the same nightmare again, but what bothered her this time was the presence of Agnivesh next to her. She didn't want to reveal her innermost demons to him. She sat up in bed and held her head for a while, then she looked up at Agnivesh and found him glaring at her incredulously.

"Don't worry. It was just a bad dream," Reeva tried to explain.

"Did you kill someone in your dream?" Agnivesh asked, and the hair on her nape stood up instantly. Her eyes widened in trepidation and panic started to twist her gut.

"How…" she trailed off. How did he know about her dreams? She looked at him tongue-tied, unsure of what to say. She noticed rage in his glossy and red rimmed eyes. But why? Perhaps she had woken him up from sleep.

"You were murmuring something like that in your sleep," Agnivesh said, reading her expressions. She exhaled deeply.

"Oh! Umm…m-maybe. I don't remember anything," she lied and averted her eyes instantly. Agnivesh kept looking at her, but she ignored him. She knew that he would read the lie in her words if she kept looking into his eyes.

"Is there something you think I should know?" he asked. She had never talked about it to anyone. She knew that she would eventually have to tell him the truth one day if she was considering this relationship, but today wasn't that day. So, she just shook her head in a 'no'.

"Is there nothing to talk about, or do you not want to talk about it?" he asked, trying to interpret her 'no'. She looked at him. He seemed determined to know the answer. Words choked her throat. A beat passed and Agnivesh quirked his brow to express that he was still waiting for her reply. She cleared her throat and said, "There is nothing to say." That was a lie, but she wasn't in a state to give him even the slightest glimpse of her past. She knew that he wouldn't understand. No one would ever understand.

He closed his eyes for a moment as if he knew that she was lying and when he opened them again, there was an enigmatic sparkle in them.

"Go back to sleep, Reeva," he ordered and with that, the softer side of Agnivesh that she had discovered only recently was gone. She slid inside the blanket and turned her back towards him.

The room was filled with sunlight when Reeva opened her eyes a few hours later. She rolled out of bed and pivoted to check the couch where Agnivesh had slept. Though he had told her initially that they would be sharing the bed, he didn't sleep with her. When she didn't find him on the couch, she spun on her heel to check the washroom. Just then, the main door clicked open and he entered the room.

"Good morning," she said hesitantly, unsure about his mood. He came close to her and brushed his fingers over her cheek. "Good morning," he smiled, and Reeva returned the smile with the same enthusiasm.

"I need to leave, I am already late," she said, feeling his touch.

"I know," he said and drew his hand back. Reeva instantly missed his touch. He leaned to one side to dig through his track pants' pocket for the keycard. Holding it up for her, he said, "This is for you."

"What is that?" she asked, though she had an inkling of what it could be.

"The key to this room. From now on, whenever you need space, you can come use it. I have permanently booked this room, and I occasionally stay here," he explained.

She could have refused his offer, but she didn't. Instead, she took the key from his hand.

"Are you sure?" she confirmed.

"Very sure," he smiled. "And one more thing, I won't be here for the next full week and may not be able to attend calls for some time. So if you need anything, just talk to Manish. You have his number, right?"

Reeva nodded and marvelled at how her opinion was changing about Agnivesh! He wasn't that tough and arrogant in reality, as he had shown himself to be earlier.

A few hours later, she was at her workshop. She sensed a change in her own demeanor. There was an extra bounce in her step and she was chirpy, calm and content. After a long time, she felt like she was smiling for real and not just for pretence; she felt like living as opposed to just surviving. Every time she opened her handbag, she didn't close it without touching the key Agnivesh had given her, and blushing. And every time she did that, she scolded herself for behaving like a teenager. She wondered how a small glimmer of hope had brought such a change in her attitude!

She opened her laptop and started to check through her emails. There was one mail that caught her attention first. It was from the Royal Exposition Mart (REM) Ltd., the organizers of the art expo she was so fervent to be part of. She quickly tapped on the mail and frowned upon reading that they had allotted a stall for *Kreative Krafts* at a premium location, and had received the full amount for the same as well. It took just a call from her to the REM office to find out where the funds had come from. But she had never told Agnivesh about her plans for this expo, then how had he come to know about it? Was he snooping in on her? A pang of annoyance started clawing at her heart. Though she had started focusing on the positive side of her impending relationship with Agnivesh, she wasn't okay with such meddling in her business. It was something very personal to her and she had always been quite possessive about it. Somewhere, she started to feel that Agnivesh was trying to flaunt his superiority over her and show her that she was nothing in comparison with him.

With rising fury, she called on his number, but it didn't connect. She decided to call Manish then, as he was the only person who could give her a clearer picture on this. She dialed his number and he answered instantly.

"Hello, Ms. Panchal. How may I help you?" Manish said.

"Umm…I want to talk to Agnivesh. When can I speak with him?" she asked.

"He is busy for the next few days. If you need anything, you can tell me. I will convey your message."

"Nothing. I don't need anything. But I certainly need some answers. Why did he make a payment to REM Ltd. on my behalf?"

"Because that was mandatory. It's one of the most prestigious expos in the city, and any delay in the payment might have caused a cancellation," Manish clarified, only to raise the fury that was already heaving in her chest.

"And who gave you the right to do it without my consent?"

"It was an order from Mr. Solanki, and the payments were made on the very same day after your meeting."

She shook her head. It was unbelievable for her that he had been prying on her activities for that long. "When can I talk to him?"

"You can give me a message, and he will call you back as soon as he gets the time."

"Okay. Tell your boss to stop snooping around my things. I am not interfering in any of his dealings, and he should respect my boundaries just the same. I know it's a little hard to understand for that hotheaded man, but tell him to stop being an asshole and limit his attention to his own business," she said, grinding her teeth in anger, and disconnected the line. She wondered what she was going to do about it now. She held her head and pressed her temples. It was difficult for her to arrange the money for a stall even at an ordinary location, and Agnivesh had paid for a premium one. She covered her face with her hands and tried to comprehend the situation. After a while, she called at the REM office again and requested them to cancel her booking against the premium location, and change it to an ordinary one. However, they refused, saying that she either had to accept this one or scrap the whole deal. It left Reeva even more exasperated. Time blurred and it was past nine in the evening when she received a call from Agnivesh.

"This is really bad. I am not going to tolerate this kind of an interference," she rumbled as soon as she picked up the phone.

"Hello Reeva, I am good. Thanks for asking. How are you?" he said sarcastically.

She closed her eyes and calmed herself down. "I am sorry. But this is not the way. You can't interfere in my business. I was dying to get that deal, but all by myself. And you proved that I couldn't have done it without your help."

"You have done it yourself, Reeva. And I am proud of you, because I know it's not easy to get in there. I just helped financially, because any delay would have led to a cancellation."

"And you presumed that I wouldn't be able to arrange the money? I had planned everything. I would have paid it myself."

"How?"

"I was going to apply for a bank loan."

"Then consider it a loan."

"But it's way too much, and I hadn't planned for a premium stall."

There was complete silence between them for a while and then she heard him sigh.

"Reeva, I don't know if you know this, but I am one of the primary sponsors of that event. We get exclusive discounts, so the amount is almost the same as what you would have paid for your preferred location. You may pay me back according to your planned budget. I am still against it, but I will accept it if it makes you feel any better."

Reeva had nothing to say after that.

"Loan? Umm...okay, a loan is fine. I think I can do it," she agreed finally.

"We are going to share our lives, Reeva. There is no harm in sharing the assets. And trust me, if I ever need your money, I won't hesitate to ask you for help."

She felt like laughing at this. Nonetheless, she appreciated his intention.

"Okay. If I ever need anything from you, I will ask for it myself, but promise me that you won't do anything like this without my knowledge."

"Fair enough. I will keep this in mind next time."

"Thanks."

"So, am I still a snoopy hotheaded asshole?"

"Oh, my God! Did he tell you everything?" she asked, surprised that Manish had actually told him everything she said. Word to word.

"He sent me a recording of the conversation."

"Really? He recorded?"

"Yes, Reeva. He knows that I like to have all my conversations recorded."

"Really? But why?"

"A few habits don't have reasons. You just do it," he said.

Reeva heard the clank of utensils on his end of the line. "Where are you?" she asked.

"I am at home."

"Oh! You must be having dinner," she said.

"Well, no. I am cooking dinner," he replied.

"You can cook?" she asked.

"Will you be impressed if I say yes?" he said, and Reeva blushed at his frivolous tone.

"Hmm, when are you coming back?" she tried to change the topic.

"Are you missing me?"

"Are you still planning to move here permanently?" she dodged his question again.

"Do I have your *yes* to my proposal?"

"You are answering all of my questions with your questions."

"Because my answers depend on your answers."

"Yes."

"Huh?"

"*Yes* is my answer to all of your questions," she said, nibbling her lip.

"I will be back, very soon. And I am moving there permanently, though it will take some time." She sensed a smile in his tone.

"I understand."

"You should sleep now, Reeva. It's late. Good night." His voice conveyed an intense command. Reeva stifled her smile in response.

"You know what, it's not mandatory to sound so bossy all the time. I mean, if we are going to share our lives, you need to be a bit polite and considerate."

"I will try my best. Now please, mademoiselle, it's too late and you must be tired. So you better go to bed soon," he warbled, and she didn't stifle her laughter this time.

"Aha! Someone knows how to joke," she said, giggling.

"You know nothing about me, Reeva. I am yet to reveal my other sides to you. Good night," he said in a stern voice and hung up the phone, leaving Reeva wondering if it was just a joke or a warning. Reeva decided to stick with the positive vibes she was experiencing being with Agnivesh. He was rude, mysterious and all that, yet there was an unknown force that constantly pulled her towards him, as if being a part of his world was no longer a desire, but a necessity. Had she started to develop feelings for him? These unnamed feelings were very new to her. In spite of all the hatred, doubts and uncertainties that she had felt earlier, he had remained in her mind, expunging all the qualms. Wasn't she already in a relationship with him? What was it if not a relationship, defined by such strong yet unnamed feelings?

***

# All About Sona

10 April, 2012

*Dear Diary,*

*Today was an amazingly amazing day because I – naah... no spoilers. Let me start from the beginning: So, as usual, I went to the sports complex today with the intention of watching her from a distance. But when I reached there, I didn't find her at the usual place where she waits for her friend. My heart sank instantly with the thought that I wouldn't see her today, but then I heard a muffled female's voice cursing in anger. When I looked in the direction of the sound, I saw her, holding a racquet in her hand and jumping to reach up to the branch of a tree. When I looked up at the tree to know why it had suddenly become her victim, I saw a shuttlecock stuck on the branch there. Why had she been practicing here? I couldn't understand. I stood there and silently watched her struggling to get it back. With a height of only five feet and four inches, when she couldn't reach the branch, she started looking around, perhaps for some help.*

*That was when her eyes landed on me. She looked at me for the first time in thirteen days, and I froze in the same spot where I stood. She kept looking at me for a few seconds, then resumed trying to reach the branch with her racquet, muttering something under her breath. When she couldn't do it still, she turned and walked towards a wall under which some bricks lay piled. She picked up two bricks and stacked them beneath the tree. She stood up on them and tried again, but she still couldn't reach it as she was unable to jump now. She looked at me again, and this time her gaze oozed with anger. Whoa! She was mad at me. Why? I hadn't put her shuttlecock there. Then she flexed her fingers at me in a gesture to call me. My legs began wobbling suddenly. I couldn't decide whether to go or run in the opposite direction. As I stood there undecided, she started hurling curse words at me. My legs automatically started taking me in her direction and before I knew it, I was standing in front of her. She placed her hands on her hips, her brows rutted and her face red from the workout she had been engaged in for some time. She looked prettier up close. I didn't say anything, but she did. And when she did, her voice seemed like music to my ears. I can still feel it reverberating in my head. She broke my daze by snapping her fingers so that I could concentrate on the lyrics. I even remember the exact words she said.*

*"You are such a jerk! What is the use of your six feet if you can't help a girl here?" she said, waving her hand up and down to indicate my height. Oh! So she wanted my help. Indeed, I am a jerk. Why hadn't it come to my mind before? Perhaps I was too busy gawking at her, or that her presence had numbed all my other senses.*

*"Now, will you please help me?" she jibed, folding her hands. I nodded and bent down, wrapped my arms around her thighs and lifted her up. She was light as a feather. I was still revelling in the moment when she suddenly started screaming. Her hands began hitting and pushing my shoulders, while her legs hammered incessantly at my thighs and knees. What had I done wrong now? I put her down and she pushed me hard. I stumbled a few steps back. I would have shoved and hit back if it was anyone else, but surprisingly, I didn't feel offended. Rather, I was worried about her annoyance.*

*"You moron! How dare you touch me?" she shouted.*

*"You-you-you..." I wanted to tell her that she only asked for my help, but I couldn't let the words out and felt mortified. I decided to distance myself from her immediately.*

*"What you, you, you? I know your kind of boys very well. Now hold it and hit that branch with it." She extended the*

*racquet that she was holding in her hand towards me. God! Why didn't I think of it before? Perhaps I really lose my senses in her presence. I hit the racquet on the branch, and with just one shot, the shuttlecock fell down.*

*"Thanks," she said nonchalantly, and I gave the racquet back to her. I turned to leave, cursing myself for having come this close to her despite knowing that I should stay away from her. I had only taken a few steps when she called after me, "Hey!"*

*I looked over my shoulder in her direction. "Do you study at this college?" she asked and I nodded. "Do you have your I-card?" she asked again and I nodded again. "Can you get me entry into the complex? Actually, I am from some other college. I come here with my friend, but she seems to have gotten late today," she said, and I nodded again in response.*

*She thanked me, her voice sounding cheerful this time. She started walking beside me. Every inch of my body felt aware of her nearness. She looked at me occasionally, but I couldn't gather the courage to return her glances. I shouldn't be near her, I kept reminding myself. I knew that I would ruin it. But nothing was in my hand, it was my destiny playing with me, and I fucking wished it were for good. I took out my I-card as we entered the complex and made a quick entry in the register. I decided to go away from her immediately and I did. She called me again, but this time, it was by my name. "Kartik..."*

*I spun on my heel, completely astonished that she had paid close attention while I was filling the details in the register. She walked towards me. Standing a foot away, she thanked me again. When I responded with a nod once more, she asked, laughing, "Don't you speak?" and I suddenly felt low. I didn't want to see her mocking or pitying me, so I turned around and started walking again. She tailed after me and started walking beside me. "Hey! Talk to me. Are you angry with me?" she kept asking, but I decided not to reply. She then scrambled and skidded ahead of me, blocking my way by stretching her hands out. I stopped and tried to reply to her in a broken sentence. I had never felt that helpless before. I wanted to leave a good impression on her, but all I could give her was my broken voice. I shook my head. Perhaps she read the vulnerability on my face. "Do you stammer?" she asked. When I didn't reply, she laughed. She was mocking me. My expressions hardened, and she instantly took the hint that I hadn't liked it.*

*"Let's be friends," she said out of nowhere. In normal circumstances, I might have felt elated upon hearing these words, but it did nothing except making me more distressed. She was being sympathetic now, but the next thing she said made me smile and adore her even more.*

*"You know, we are perfect. We'll make a perfect couple. I mean, perfect friend-couple," she corrected herself. "You know, I too have a speech problem just like you. I talk too much, and that's the reason no friend stays in my life for long. If we become friends, I can do the talking on your behalf as well, and you can listen," she rocked herself to and fro as she talked.*

*"What say?" she wriggled her brows at me and a smile crept onto my face. She was exactly what I had imagined. Bubbly. Notorious. Feisty.*

*"Kriti," someone called from behind. I looked over her shoulder and found Gayatri standing with Vikrant there. They both had a scowl on their faces that told me that they didn't like her talking to me. I returned my gaze to the girl standing in front of me.*

*"Kriti, that's my name. So, friends?" She extended her hand and I took it instantly. I looked at our joined hands. My*

*hand seemed to have engulfed her small hand.*

*Kriti. Didn't I say before that she must have a unique name? And is it just a coincidence that her name sounds so well next to mine? Kriti-Kartik.*

*She turned towards her friends, while I kept looking at her, wondering whether she would talk to me again tomorrow.*

~

# 7

A whole week had passed since Reeva last met Agnivesh. They didn't chat for hours over the phone as a typical couple does after getting engaged. Their conversations over the phone were short and to the point. They weren't going to be like other couples, Reeva had accepted this fact. No official engagement ceremony was held, as Agnivesh wasn't in favor of it, and told her parents to fix the wedding date directly. Her parents had already started running from one astrologer to another for the most auspicious date for the wedding. It irked Reeva that they were consulting so many astrologers, but she didn't try to stop them. It wasn't new. The first time her parents ever visited an astrologer was when she had left her studies and decided to confine herself. They were so worried then and had been doing the same since, running to astrologers as if they would be able to cure her with their *tantra-mantra*. She picked up her lunch box along with the water bottle from the dining table and put them in her handbag. She had just turned towards the shoe rack to grab her sandals when her mother called her. "Reeva, can you take an off tomorrow?"

"Why?" Reeva asked, not paying much attention to her mother's request.

"Because I am asking you to. Isn't that reason enough?"

"No. Now please, stop playing these games and tell me why," asked Reeva, looking at her mother this time. Sumitra hesitated for a moment and wriggled her hands, which told Reeva that her mother was about to say something that she may not like.

"Umm...we have consulted many astrologers, and they all have suggested that we must conduct a puja before fixing the wedding date," her mother tried to elucidate, but the nervousness in her voice pushed Reeva to the edge. Reeva closed her eyes in exasperation. She was tired of the involvement of these astrologers and the repeated weird pujas, but she did everything for the sake of her parents' happiness.

"What kind of puja and why?"

"Actually, there is a *mangal dosha* in your *kundali* and... you know, there is a remedy...many people do it..." Her mother's voice trailed off, making Reeva feel even more skeptical about it.

"Maa, don't beat around the bush and tell me the truth."

"Remember, a famous actress did this too...it was on the news. All you have to do is marry a tree and then they will destroy it. It's nothing and will hardly take an hour," her mother said, laughing nervously. Reeva clenched her hands into fists, fury starting to surge in her chest. She quickly spun on her heel, put on her sandals and opened the main door to leave.

"I may not come home for the next two days," Reeva said before storming out of the house. Her mother kept calling after her, but she didn't entertain her. She kept walking briskly. She couldn't tell whether she was angry because of her parents' behavior or her own helplessness. What kind of a fate had she got? It kept playing games with her, turning her life into a joke where she was the punchline. Soon, she reached the main gate and hailed for an Auto. Through the entire ride to her workshop, she tried hard not to think about the information her mother had just barraged her with. How could they even consider that? Wasn't there a lawsuit against such a thing? And more importantly, how could a parent mortify their kid by doing that? She was hurt and in pain, but she put on a smile on her face as soon as the Auto stopped in front of her workshop.

She indulged herself in work and made her mind too occupied to think about anything else. She had learnt to make herself a priority, not because she was a narcissist, but as a necessity for her own survival. She carried through the whole day quite well, but as dusk drew closer, she started getting cold feet. Other people began to leave the workshop one by one, and soon she was left all alone. It wasn't the first time she was spending the night here, but just like every other time, it scared her being alone in that secluded place. Her mind kept coaxing her to leave, as unlike before, she had an option this time. She opened her handbag and took out the hotel room key card that Agnivesh had given her. The thought tempted her, but she hesitated. Would Agnivesh like her using his room when he wasn't around? Questions started soaring in her mind, but she dismissed them. He would never have given her the keys if he hadn't intended her to use it. She eventually made up her mind and hurried out before it got too late to get a ride.

It took her hardly ten minutes to get there. Once inside, she straightaway took the elevator, punched her keycard there and pushed the button for the desired floor. She kept rubbing the knuckles of her hands till she found herself standing in front of the door to his suite. She lifted her hand to punch the card at the door, but stopped midway as a new thought tugged at her senses. What if she opened the door and found him inside the room? But then she remembered him telling her that he wouldn't be back until the next week, and even if he was there in the room, it was time to catch him red-handed. She tapped the card at the door and unlocked it.

It was dark inside. She pushed the card into the socket and the room got flooded with light. The entire place was spotless and untouched. She heaved a sigh of relief because of two reasons: one, he wasn't there; and two, he hadn't been lying to her. She placed her handbag on the table and headed towards the washroom to freshen up. Since it wasn't a planned night out, she hadn't got any clothes to change into for the night. She went into the large dressing room and opened a wardrobe. His fragrance assaulted her senses instantly. His shirts were hanging inside, all neatly ironed and lined up. She pulled out a drawer to find some of his T-shirts and sweatpants inside, all nicely folded. She carefully took out a set and strolled towards the washroom. His clothes hung comically over her body, as she was almost five-sizes down compared to Agnivesh. She decided against using his nicely made bed and made herself comfortable on the couch that lay in the corner of the room. She was so exhausted that as soon as she lied down, darkness took over her consciousness and she fell into deep slumber.

The sun was peeking through the full-length window when she opened her eyes the next morning. She pulled her hands out of the smooth white comforter and rolled over the soft mattress that felt as fluffy as a cloud. Relishing the comfort, she pulled a soft pillow from the other side of the bed towards herself and hugged it.

Bed? Pillow? Mattress? That damn comforter? Hadn't she slept on the couch the previous night? Her eyes flipped open and she sat up hurriedly, looking here and there for a clue. Did she walk while sleeping? But she had never done that before. She was still in a daze when a voice startled her.

"Don't be so surprised, Reeva. It was I who tucked you in bed." The voice had come from the sitting area and he appeared in front of her soon after, holding a cup of tea. Reeva was too shocked to say anything. He closed the distance, kept the teacup on the side table and sat beside, facing her. He leaned forward and kissed her forehead.

"Good morning," he said.

"Good morning to you too," Reeva said after clearing her throat. "How come you are here?" she asked.

"The moment you entered this room, I knew that you needed me. So I am here, and I am all ears. What happened?" Agnivesh asked, brushing his fingers lightly over her cheek. She closed her eyes momentarily to revel in his touch, but soon came back to the conversation.

"I have some *dosha* in my *kundali*, and my parents want me to do weird things to get rid of that," she said, while he listened to her attentively. He took a moment before replying, "Do you believe in these things?"

"No," she replied.

"Neither do I. You need not do anything you don't believe in. Don't worry. Nothing will happen against your wish,"—he paused for a moment to study her expressions—"Not even this wedding. And I mean it," he said, looking into her eyes. At that moment, she knew that she had fallen a little more for him. She felt an assurance and honesty in his voice that promised her an enduring future. She smiled genially and nodded.

"I have to go to work," she whispered.

"I know," he replied and stood up to give her space to clamber off the bed. She rose from the bed and instantly grabbed the pants she was wearing, as they were too loose for her. She looked up at Agnivesh and found him hiding his amusement behind his fingers.

"Are you making fun of me?" she asked.

"No. But you seem like you're swimming in my clothes. Why don't I remember offering you my clothes?"

"You didn't. I just made myself at home," Reeva replied.

"I am glad you did. You have no idea how happy I am to see you here."

"And I was worrying you would think me a clingy girl."

"It'll be a privilege for me, Reeva."

"You know what, no one has ever made me feel this special. Why are you doing this? Why does every word you say hit me so hard? Instead of hurting, it heals me," she said, genuinely overwhelmed by his gestures.

"Why don't I believe you?" he asked, looking into her eyes. There was a sense of incredulity in his voice. "I mean, how is it possible that no one has ever made you feel special?" he corrected himself.

"Perhaps I am not good enough for people. I have a past, Agnivesh, that I am not very proud of," she spurted out the words that had been lingering on her tongue for quite long.

"I know. You carry it like a baggage every day, and I will be happy to share it if you allow me to… someday, when you are ready to share it." His words fell like a drop of rain over her parched heart. He smiled and its upshot reflected on her face too.

"What will you have for breakfast?" he asked, changing the topic.

"I will have something on my way to the workshop," she replied.

"Did you have dinner yesterday?"

"No."

"Then you aren't leaving this place without breakfast. I am ordering some french toast, oatmeal and stuffed *parathas*. Is that fine?"

"Sounds perfect," she smiled and walked towards the washroom.

Soon after, the breakfast was served on the table. Agnivesh was feasting on the meal leisurely, while Reeva gobbled on it as fast as she could.

"Eat slow, Reeva," Agnivesh ordered, and Reeva automatically slowed down a bit.

"I am in a hurry," she said.

"I can see that," he looked at her for a moment, then whispered, "May I expect you here tonight as well?"

"Do you want me here?" Reeva whispered in response.

He nodded, his gaze still locked with Reeva's, and she instantly felt the heebie-jeebies deep in her gut. When was the last she had felt that way? She couldn't recollect, for the feeling seemed new to her. The man sitting in front of her undoubtedly held some power over her. She averted her eyes, realizing she was giving away a piece of her with every latch of their gazes.

"I will send a car for you in the evening," Agnivesh said. Reeva couldn't resist the offer and smiled in response.

An hour passed, she reached her workshop and busied herself in work. There was again an order for handmade wedding invitation cards and return gifts. She knew that it was time to increase her workforce because of her growing business, but finding good artisans was itself a task. Though she had interviewed a few people, they hadn't met her expectations. She was new to this business, so getting experienced ones was difficult, while the rest were too amateurish. She posted again on her Facebook and Instagram page that they were hiring. A buzz on her phone caught her attention and an instant smile spread on her face upon seeing Agnivesh's name flashing on the screen.

"Hello," she surprised herself with the way she warbled the word.

"You sound happy!" Agnivesh said. Was she? She thought for a moment and realized that it was just his call that had made her happy for the moment.

"I am," she replied, smiling audibly.

"Did you talk to your mother?" he asked out of nowhere.

"Umm…no."

"You should. She must be waiting for your call. It's her birthday," he said, and Reeva instantly pressed her temples, realizing that she had completely forgotten her mother's birthday.

"I will do it now," she said, feeling sorry.

"Hmm…and I am assuming that our meeting today is annulled as you will be visiting your parents."

"Umm…yeah." Her heart was swamped by waves of displeasure, thinking about not seeing him again that day.

"Bye, talk to you later," he said and terminated the call. Reeva kept the handset glued to her ear as if she was still conversing with him in her head. Suddenly, an idea flashed in her mind and she redialed his number. He took the call on the first ring.

"Hey, I was thinking, why don't you join us for dinner today? Mom will be happy to see you there," she said.

"Umm…I will have to check my schedule," he said and she heard the sound of papers ruffling in the background. She realized that he must be in some meeting.

"Please. For me." Reeva was surprised to hear her own voice sounding so desperate.

"Done. I'll be there at seven," he said and exhaled a sigh, "See you then."

***

# All About Sona

11 April, 2012

*Dear Diary,*

*I saw her today too, at the same spot and at the same time. Her cousin wasn't late today, so I didn't get much time to watch her. I was about to leave when she saw me and called me by my name. My name sounds so different in her voice; it induces a sensation in my body that I can't even explain. When I looked at her, she waved at me, and I responded with a wave too. Then, she whispered something in her cousin's ear and rushed towards me. She was smiling the whole time as she sprinted towards me and I couldn't believe my stars. She was smiling at me, and that's new. Otherwise, I am more habitual of people scowling at me.*

*"Are you free?" she asked me, panting. I nodded, and she smiled. "Then come with me, I get bored as I have no friends here," she added. That moment was the toughest for me; my heart told me to go with her, while my brain refused. Perhaps I took too much time to decide because the next moment, I found her dragging me by the arm. My arm is still tingling with the sensation of her touch, and no matter how cliche it sounds, I haven't washed my arm yet. I am afraid that the feel of her hand would go as soon as I wash it off.*

*"C'mon, stop being pigheaded. I know you want to come," she said as she pulled me.*

*Pigheaded? Really? I am still laughing thinking about the way she called me that. We headed to the cafeteria near the sports complex and sat there for the entire evening. And I tell you, when she said that she had a speech problem, she wasn't lying. Man! She talks non-stop. She spoke about her college, her friends and her friends' friends. I kept listening to her. She also told me that Gayatri is in a relationship with Vikrant. I didn't tell her that I already knew that. She comes with Gayatri here so that Gayatri may spend some time with him. They lie at home that they come here for practicing badminton. While they spend their time together, she goes to the library. She was happy to have found me as now she wouldn't get bored anymore. She also asked me if I would come tomorrow and I happily nodded. She is a good girl, and I don't see any reason to be rude to her, neither to stay away from her.*

*So the news is, I am going to see her tomorrow too. I am happy.*

~

# 8

"Just calm down, Maa." Reeva tried to appease her mother who had been running here and there since the moment she came to know that Agnivesh would be joining them for dinner. "Don't be so formal, he won't even notice anything, he is just like us."

"You know nothing, Reeva. You should have told me about this the moment he told you that he would be coming here," her mother said, removing the covers of cushions apprehensively.

"I wanted to surprise you. I thought you'd be happy to have him join us. If I had known it was going to make you so anxious, I would have dodged him."

"I am not anxious. It's just that I want to make him feel the same comfort that he has at his own home. His lifestyle is entirely different from us"—she stopped talking abruptly and her hands paused for a moment as though thinking about something, then she added—"What if he feels that we are too mediocre in comparison with him. I don't want to give him a reason to recoil." Saying this, she resumed her work.

"Why do you think that he will recoil? He won't. Trust me, I know him enough now. He is a nice person," Reeva said and her mother's eyes darted towards her as if she had said something unimaginable. Reeva knew that it was the words *'I know him enough now'* that were rattling in her mother's ears. She hadn't told her mother anything regarding the nights she had spent with Agnivesh. Suddenly, her mother's lips quirked up in a smile and her eyes twinkled. "You can't even imagine how happy I am right now. Didn't I say this already? Luck has knocked at your door, and you have realized this too now."

Reeva smiled. Didn't she realize how her life and her behavior had changed since Agnivesh entered it? She wasn't herself when she was around Agnivesh; as if he had some magical powers that made her forget the things that had haunted her every time she took a breath. But now, she had started living again, more than just breathing. She had begun to look forward to the future, and not just in terms of her business. The thought of sharing a place with Agnivesh that they would call home made her stomach flutter in a way that she had completely forgotten. No matter how many times she denied it, her conscience knew that she was in love and that she had started envisaging a future. A 'happily-ever-after' kind of future. Her life had finally started to come back on track.

The ding of the doorbell hauled Reeva out of her reverie and both the ladies snapped their heads to look at the watch. It was seven dot. Another thing Reeva had learnt about Agnivesh was that he hated being late and was always on time. Reeva rushed to open the door and there he was, standing tall. He wore a grey tailored fit suit. This was the first time she was seeing him in his office wear. He looked at Reeva with a little amazed expression. She had adorned herself for him for the first time too. She wore a plain black sleeveless dress that ended a little above her knees. Her long hair were swept to one shoulder and cascaded down to her waist in soft loose curls. Agnivesh took his time to drink her in and when he finally looked back into her eyes, his expression transformed into an appreciative grin. "You look beautiful," he said. Reeva's cheeks reddened in response. Her mother coughed from behind and teased, "Are you both just going to stare at each other, or do you have any plans to come in?"

Reeva moved aside, clearing the doorway for Agnivesh. As Agnivesh entered, Reeva saw that he was holding a bouquet that she hadn't noticed earlier. Perhaps she had been too busy gawking at him.

"Wish you a very happy birthday, Mrs. Panchal," Agnivesh said, extending the bouquet towards her mother. She took it happily and thanked him for the gesture.

"Now you should develop the habit of calling me Maa, just as Reeva does," Sumitra said.

"I will keep that in mind. Where is Mr. Panchal?" Agnivesh asked.

"He has gone to buy the birthday cake," Reeva replied and sat on the arm of the sofa, while Agnivesh took a seat on the sofa chair. Soon, Reeva's father arrived with the birthday cake and Sumitra cut the cake. Throughout dinner, Reeva noticed that Agnivesh kept checking his watch, which made Reeva realize how she had forced him to come here. Though he was present there physically, mentally he was still working. Reeva served him the dessert and leaned forward to whisper in his ear, "I am sorry, I shouldn't have forced you to come here."

Agnivesh studied her for a while, then asked, "Why did you say that?"

"I think you really had something important on your plate and I just pulled you here. That's why you are checking your watch now and then," she replied.

“Ah! It’s not what you are thinking,” Agnivesh said and tapped on the arm of the sofa chair, signaling her to sit close to him. She perched herself there instantly.

“I am waiting for someone. I came here straight from the office and didn’t get any time to bring something for Mrs. Panchal, so I gave the responsibility to Manish. He should be arriving here anytime,” he elucidated.

“Oh!” Reeva said, realizing how little she understood him! Why did she always presume the worst? She shook her head to clear her mind.

“You brought flowers, and trust me, that was more than enough. You don’t have to bring any gift. Moreover, she is elated to have you here.” She nodded towards her mother who was busy serving dessert to Prakash with a big and bright smile on her face.

“You make her happy,” Reeva whispered.

“What about you?” Agnivesh asked, making Reeva realize that she had said the last part out loud. She turned her gaze towards Agnivesh. “You make me feel, and that makes me blissful…and scared, both at the same time,” she whispered. Agnivesh looked at her in confusion and was about to say something when Reeva’s parents joined them in the living room.

“What’s going on here?” Sumitra asked, narrowing her eyes mischievously at both of them.

“Nothing, we were just discussing the possible wedding dates,” Agnivesh lied and Reeva looked at him instantly, confused at where he was taking this conversation. Sumitra and Prakash glanced at each other furtively. Agnivesh studied them for a while, then said, “Reeva has told me everything about the *dosha* and *puja*. It’s our mutual decision that we aren’t going to do that, as we don’t believe in such things.”

"She told you?" Sumitra asked Agnivesh, but looked at Reeva. Reeva shrugged in response.

"Yes," Agnivesh replied.

"Well! It's important for a happy married life. We would never have insisted on it if it weren't crucial. We consulted almost every astrologer in the city, and they all came up with just this one solution. You can't take the *pheras* and vows without this puja," Sumitra explained.

"Then we won't take the *pheras*," Agnivesh said, and all the three pairs of eyes in the room darted towards him. "I mean, we won't do it in that way," Agnivesh corrected himself, then looked at Reeva. "How about a court marriage?"

"I am more than fine with that," Reeva replied instantly.

"No!" Sumitra exclaimed. "We are Hindus and we have relative here. This wedding has to happen with all the rituals and as per our tradition."

"If that's the case, then I won't mind changing my religion too." He looked back at Reeva and asked, "How about marrying in a church, Reeva?"

Reeva's mind instantly envisioned them kissing, she dressed in a white gown, while Agnivesh in a black tux.

"Reeva?" Agnivesh asked again.

"I won't mind," Reeva replied, pursing her lips.

"It's decided then. We are going to have a Catholic wedding."

"This is not a joke," Prakash's stern voice jolted them all, but Agnivesh stood his ground firmly.

"Yes, that's what I am trying to say. This is not a joke. Foisting something on her that she is not comfortable with in the name of religion is definitely not a joke," Agnivesh said, and a sudden rush of emotions gushed over Reeva's heart. She hadn't expected him to stand for her, yet he cared about her opinion and was even fighting with her parents for her. Suddenly, she realized how easy life becomes if you have someone by your side to fight your battles.

"This puja is to remove all the hindrances that may come in your life after the wedding..." Sumitra tried to explain, but Agnivesh cut her off. "At the moment, this puja itself is the biggest hindrance in the way of the wedding. We can't control our fate, but if two people are determined to spend their life together, no *dosha* can keep them apart."

Sumitra looked down, then said after chewing the cud, "Whatever you feel is appropriate. If she doesn't want this puja, we won't force her, but this wedding will happen according to our customs and traditions."

Reeva's smile widened. It was so easy to persuade her parents, yet she had always chosen to run instead of talking. Perhaps it wouldn't have been that easy if Agnivesh hadn't stepped in. It had once happened earlier too when she had given in to do something weird that her parents had told her to do. She shook her head to efface the memory of it and looked at Agnivesh adoringly. She realized that God had his own ways to connect people who were made for each other. The buzz of the doorbell caught everyone's attention just then. Both Reeva and Agnivesh stood up at the same time to get the door, but Agnivesh requested Reeva to remain seated.

"I know who it is," he said and sauntered towards the main door. Soon, he returned with a commercial sized envelope in his hand and handed it over to Sumitra.

"What is this?" Sumitra asked astounded.

"Your birthday gift," Agnivesh replied.

Sumitra opened it and found some printed stamp papers inside. It didn't take her much time to realize what those documents were. She gasped as soon as she read them and passed them on to Prakash. Reeva looked at them ardently, trying to grasp what was there in those papers.

"Why did you do that? We can't take this from you. It's huge," Sumitra said. Reeva looked at her, still unaware of what the papers meant. She circled the sofa to reach her father who was reading the papers now.

"Of course you can, if you want me to call you *maa*," he replied.

"But still, it's—" she started, but Agnivesh cut her off again. "I don't believe in those relations whose scope is limited only to the names. If you really consider me your son, you have to consider this too."

"You bought this flat?" Reeva came close to Agnivesh and asked, holding up the papers.

"I couldn't find any other appropriate gift," he answered in a matter-of-fact way.

"And so you bought this flat? Seriously? We can't take this. It's too much," Reeva said.

"This is not for you, Reeva. If Mrs. Panchal asks me to take it back, I'll take it," Agnivesh said, looking at Sumitra.

"Thanks. I'll accept it as you are giving it to me as a son. I don't have words to tell you how grateful I am feeling right now." Sumitra's eyes pooled with tears. "Since the day I got married, I have had only one dream—to have my own house. But destiny had something else in store and I had almost given up on that wish. Whenever I looked at Reeva"—she averted her gaze to look at Reeva—"I always thought that things would have been different had she been a boy. But today, you have proved that it's not necessary for a son to be born from your womb"—she raised her hand and caressed Agnivesh's cheek—"A son-in-law can be your son too."

Reeva's eyes welled up at her mother's confession, but the only thing that irked her was Agnivesh's reaction to her mother's display of affection. He had a frown on his face as if he wasn't comfortable. Perhaps he wasn't habitual of being fondled, as he had himself admitted that he left his home long ago and had no interaction with his family.

Agnivesh and Prakash took their seat on the sofa and started chatting, while Reeva helped her mother clear up the empty dishes on the dining table. Prakash was curious to know how Agnivesh had achieved such a fantastic success in such a short span, and Agnivesh was elated to discuss his struggle. A sound of laughter filled the house and they both turned their heads towards its source. Sumitra was whispering something in Reeva's ear and Reeva was giggling in response. The sound was usual for Agnivesh, but Prakash's eyes remained glued to the panorama. A slow smile touched his lips and his eyes started to gloss. Blinking the tears away, he looked back at Agnivesh who was attentively noticing Prakash's mien.

"Do you hear this sound?" Prakash asked Agnivesh, gesturing towards Reeva. "We had entirely forgotten this sound. It's been four years since she laughed out loud like this."

"What happened four years back?" Agnivesh prodded.

"She didn't take her grandfather's death well. I still remember that fateful day. It was the same day she met with an accident while coming home by auto. She had a wound on the side of her forehead and bruises all over her body. She was still in trauma when she had to face the truth about her grandfather's demise. She was very fond of him and took his death in a hard way."

"What day was this?" Agnivesh asked.

"22 May, 2012," he paused for a moment, as if ruminating that ill-fated day, then looked back at Agnivesh admiringly. "You've made her happy again. You know, I was skeptical about this relationship. Even till earlier today, I wasn't sure. But you proved me wrong and I really can't thank you enough," he said as he joined his hands in front of Agnivesh who held them instantly and shook his head, embarrassed by Prakash's gesture.

Reeva's gaze flew to the scene in front of her, her father's joined hands and glossy eyes, and Agnivesh's demeanor. Though she couldn't hear anything because of the distance, she knew that some serious conversation was going on. She pivoted towards them and looked on incredulously, darting her gaze from her father to Agnivesh and back.

Agnivesh caught her eye and answered quickly, "I was just telling him that I need to leave now."

"Why so early? Stay for some more time," Sumitra chimed in.

"No. I can't. My flight to Mumbai is due in the next three hours," he replied.

"Oh!" Sumitra couldn't argue further. Reeva looked at him disappointedly. She hadn't expected him to leave this early. What kind of a relationship were they going to have? Reeva wondered. When he was with her, he seemed so much into her as though she was the axis of his universe, and once he left, he was as distant and aloof as could be. That was the reason why Reeva was disappointed. Somewhere, she knew that this distance was a hindrance in their blooming relationship, but she couldn't stop him. Despite the little comfort they had built, she still felt she didn't have the right to stop him. At least, she could try…

"I will walk you down," she offered instantly. Agnivesh nodded and took his leave. Reeva escorted him holding a torch, as it was dark outside and the corridor's lights were yet to be switched on. Once they were on the road, Reeva started the conversation, "Thanks for coming and the big gift. Maa is so thrilled."

He nodded and gave her a side-glance. "And you?" he asked, sliding his hands in the pockets of his pants.

"Super happy," she said elatedly, and his lips curved into a smile. Reeva's smile soon faded as she caught sight of his car parked at the curb.

"When will you be here next?" she asked as they stopped to say a final goodbye to each other.

"I have no idea. It depends on when the business needs me here..." he shrugged and then added, "Or you." Reeva smiled meekly at him, unable to form a sentence that could bespeak her sentiments precisely. Agnivesh gave her a quick side hug and a kiss on the side of her head, then sauntered towards his car. His driver had already opened the door for him and he was about to slide in when Reeva called after him, "Agnivesh."

He stopped immediately and gestured his driver to take his seat. Reeva ambled towards him and put her arms around his neck. Raising herself on her toes, she gave him a quick peck on his lips and whispered, "I'll miss you. Do come soon, and don't forget to call me daily." She slid down her hands and snaked them around his waist, hugging him tightly. Reeva sensed the way Agnivesh's body stiffened. She noticed that he kept his hands at his sides and didn't hug her back. A pang of unknown emotion gushed through her heart, and suddenly she felt dejected. She loosened her grip and was about to step back when Agnivesh surprised her by holding her tight against his chest. Reeva's gut fluttered at the feel of his tight chest and firm arms around her.

"Sure," he responded. She looked up at him as he kissed her forehead.

She was surprised at her own display of affection. She had never done that before. This was what he had done to her. She felt alive again, and so she didn't hesitate to embrace the happiness that stood at her doorstep but was in a quandary to enter her life.

***

# All About Sona

12 April, 2012

*Dear Diary,*

*Today, the whole day, I had a bounce in my step. You know why? Because when I arrived at the sports complex today, I saw her waiting outside. And this time, she wasn't waiting for anyone else but me. She beamed as soon as she saw me and I swear, I felt my stomach dropping. This is how I feel around her. Different. Something raw and unexplored.*

*"I was waiting for you," she trilled as she saw me approaching her. "Let's go to the cafeteria, I am so hungry today," she said, holding my arm and pulling me towards the cafeteria. Once we were seated inside the cafeteria, she looked at me squeamishly.*

*"What?" I asked.*

*She just shook her head and started exploring the menu. Though she tried to keep her gaze on the menu, her eyes danced here and there furtively. Then, I caught her looking at someone sitting behind me, and when I turned to look, I found the same guy whom she had been gawking at for quite some time. Raunak Patel. I couldn't stop myself from asking her if she knew him. She said that they used to be in the same school but in different sections. So she knew him, but had never talked to him. She didn't say anything else, neither did I prod any further. I considered informing her about his relationship status, but as soon as I opened my mouth, I made a blunder.*

*"Sona..." I was halted in my tracks as soon as this word escaped my mouth. I instantly bit the inside of my cheek, hoping she hadn't heard the nickname I had given her. Her eyes rose from the menu and darted towards me promptly. Her brows arched up, and I could clearly see the big question mark in her wide eyes. From the look of her, I knew that I*

*had landed myself in trouble. She had heard what I had just called her.*

*"What did you just say?"*

*"Umm...nothing," I stuttered.*

*She got up from her seat and beckoned me to follow her. That instant, I knew that she was going to scold me about this, but I felt thankful that instead of creating a scene in the cafeteria, she had called me out. As soon as we came out, she turned and faced me.*

*"See"—she pointed a finger at me—"I agreed to spend time with you, but that doesn't mean you can give me nicknames. I know what are you trying to do. This is just a trick so that you may brag in front of your friends that you have got a girlfriend like me. But let me tell you, don't you dare call me that. Ever. Our friendship is just at an infant stage, and it may go either way if you don't have control over your thoughts. It'll be better if you call me Kriti. Just Kriti," she declared. Whoa! Infant-stage-friends! Is there anything like that at all?*

*"K-k-k...K-Kriti," I said, and she grimaced.*

*"God! Call me whatever you want to, but not Kriti. The way you are calling my name, it reminds me of Rahul from the movie Darr. That character was quite scary," she said, and we both laughed. "I hate the psychos," she added, and her words hit me hard. What if one day she comes to know how violent I can be! Would she call me a psycho too? Would she still stay with me? Despair started clouding my mind, but I brushed it off instantly, keeping my focus on the sound of her laughter. See, I feel so calm and relaxed with her. I never feel bad when she makes fun of my stutter, neither does she make me feel miserable about my shortcoming. We went back to the cafeteria, and today I got to know all about her favorite dishes, colors, movies, songs, actors, players and what not. Humph! I just listened to her, dreading that saying*

*anything would spoil the moment. There is so much I want to tell her, but with this damn stammering! I have to sum everything up in one sentence. I feel helpless. And do you know, diary, you are my emotional succor. I write everything in you, so that one day she may read how I felt about her all this time. And I really wish for that day to come soon.*

~

# 9

"Yes! We have done it," exclaimed Reeva and all the four pairs of eyes in the room turned towards her, while her eyes stayed glued to the screen of her laptop.

"What happened?" asked Radhika, leaving her work and ambling towards Reeva.

"I had sent the proposal to some leading stores in Surat, and two of them have agreed to keep our products in their stores. Isn't that amazing?" said Reeva, without expecting anyone to answer. She felt giddy with delight. This was the other milestone that she had achieved in the past six months. First being the allotment of a stall for *Kreative Krafts* at REM Ltd. Expo.

"I think we should celebrate," Radhika expressed her happiness, clasping her hands and twirling on her heel.

"No. I think we should start looking for more workforce, otherwise we are going to end soon," Reeva answered, going through the responses of her recruitment advertisement. "And I don't think this advertising thing is working for us. We need to look for people personally," she added, curling her lower lip in disappointment.

"Shall I put it up on my college group?" asked Radhika, while Reeva considered it. In her small team, Radhika was the only one who had a professional degree in Fine Arts. In fact, Radhika was the only one who had any degree at all.

"I think that would be a better idea. Do it as soon as possible," Reeva told her and got engrossed in responding to her emails again. Soon after, she started collecting her things as she had to leave early for a meeting with the manager of one of the stores that had agreed to give *Kreative Krafts* a corner for their products in their store. It was already half past six in the evening, so Reeva told Radhika to close the workshop and keep the keys with her. She also made a mental note to get a duplicate set of keys made for her workshop. The last time she had asked Radhika to keep the workshop keys, she ended up in a hotel room with Agnivesh.

She blushed at the memory and thanked God that it happened, otherwise she would never have gotten to know Agnivesh the way she knew him now. It had been nine days since she saw him last and he had told her that he wouldn't be back for another week. He did call her daily, but the call never lasted more than two minutes. The one thing she had realized about Agnivesh was that despite being caring and understanding, he wasn't very expressive. He never shared his feelings or any other details about himself unless Reeva asked for it and surprisingly, she was intrigued by this enigmatic personality he had.

As she came out, the cab she had called for was already waiting at the curb. She slid in and the driver pulled away. The traffic was surprisingly light, considering the hour. She reckoned the total time she needed for this meeting and realized that it would be late by the time it got over. She pulled out her phone from the handbag and dialed her mother's number to inform her that she would be late. She knew that her parents weren't comfortable with her late arrivals every other day, and this was another reason they weren't happy with her business. She had to ignore them every time. It's not easy to follow the path you have chosen for yourself; you have to let the dreams that your loved ones may have seen for you crumble, and it was painful for her. She leaned back, rested her head on the headrest and closed her eyes. She jerked forward as the driver suddenly pulled the breaks at the red light. She straightened her back and gazed out the window. It was the time of Navratri and the whole city was gleaming with lights and zeal.

She used to be so enthusiastic for this time of the year, all until one day when everything changed. '*Don't go there, Reeva,*' she told herself and concentrated on the panorama outside the car window. It was then that her eyes landed straight on the black car. Not any other car, but Agnivesh's car. She recognized its number instantly. Someone was sitting in the back seat, but she could only see the silhouette as the glass in the windows was tinted. However, she was well acquainted with his silhouette too by now. Her gut twisted in trepidation. Though she had no reason to doubt Agnivesh, she felt cheated. He was here, though he had lied that he wouldn't be for another few days.

Impetuously, she told the driver to follow the black Porsche. The driver tailed behind Agnivesh's car, and soon they were on Hazira road. A shuddering fear spread all over her face, turning it white, as she gazed at the road they were heading on. It was the same road she had been on on that fateful day, and suddenly she dreaded the destination. She closed her eyes and waited. If the car stopped at about a hundred meters, it would be the same place she had been seeing in her nightmares. A painful hunch pervaded her senses as the car stopped as per her anticipation. She squeezed her eyes even harder, as if keeping them shut would change the reality. She opened her eyes and looked outside, only to see the hotel *The Grand Rajvilaas*. She gathered her composure as she saw Agnivesh stepping off the car and heading towards the entrance of the hotel. She turned to open the door of her cab and got down, but stopped in her tracks, thinking about entering that hotel once again. The last time she had gone inside it, a part of her died forever. Brushing everything aside, she quickly climbed down and rushed towards Agnivesh's car. She caught up to it before the driver could pull it towards the parking.

"Hi," she said, panting.

"Oh! Hello, Ma'am. I just dropped Mr. Solanki here," he sputtered.

"I know. He messaged me to come here. I was just checking if he is still in the car," she lied.

"No. He is not," the driver answered.

"Is there something special inside? I mean, why did he choose this hotel particularly?" she tried to prod.

"Umm…he owns this property, and he has been coming here for the last five days for a conference. Today is the last day," he said. Reeva froze on the spot. She was right that he had been lying to her. She didn't believe her instincts that had been shouting since the day she first met him. He had lied that he didn't own any hotel in Surat. He had lied that he was in Mumbai. Perhaps he never left for Mumbai. The honking from another car hauled her out of her trance, and she beckoned to the driver to go ahead.

She pivoted towards the entrance of the hotel. A part of her heart stopped her from confronting him right away; a part of her heart tried to coax her to wait until the next day; a part of her heart reiterated that there might be some compulsion due to which he couldn't tell her, but she was no more a pawn of her heart. It was her mind that she was listening too. As she reached the reception, she informed the receptionist that she was one of the guests of Agnivesh Solanki, and the receptionist guided her towards the function hall where an extravagant party was going on. Though her eyes were dry, her insides screamed as she read the name of the host on display outside the function hall. *Agnivesh Solanki.* The one she had started considering as family didn't care enough to tell her about the event in their city, let alone invite her.

"Ma'am, this way." The voice of the receptionist brought her back to the present. As she entered, she started feeling terribly underdressed amidst the elite of the city. While everyone else was dressed in designer clothes, she was wearing a simple jeans with a cotton Kurti. A little voice in her head told her to turn back, and this time she listened. She realized that she knew nothing about Agnivesh, his lifestyle, his routine, his regime or his friends. What was she even doing here? Suddenly, the man whom she had started seeing as a significant part of her life, felt a stranger. She had just begun to turn when her gaze caught a glimpse of Agnivesh. He was standing there surrounded by a few other people. His posture exuded confidence; his gesture oozed superiority. The way he was dressed, the way he was holding a glass of wine in his hand, rather his whole personality screamed affluence. He looked unapproachable to her. Her lower lip trembled because of the turmoil her mind was experiencing. Why was she feeling so emotional for a person she hardly knew? How did this person gain the power to hurt her? It was indeed her fault. People can affect us, hurt us or make us feel worthless, only if we give them the power to do so. She kept a check on her tears. Hell! If she ever let him see how he was affecting her! She took a step back while her eyes remained glued to him. When she took another step back, Agnivesh finally looked at her, as if he could sense her gaze on him, but could he sense her state? Perhaps, yes. Reeva noticed the swift change in his expressions, and that gave her enough courage to confront him. Putting more confidence in her walk, she padded towards him. Soon, she was standing in front of him with her gaze locked with his. All the other people standing there looked at them dubiously.

Agnivesh hesitated for a moment, but soon pulled himself together. He cleared his throat before addressing the people around him, "Excuse me, please. Umm...a friend of mine is here. I just need a few minutes."

*'A friend of mine'* These words reverberated in Reeva's mind. Her heart sank thinking about the way Agnivesh had introduced her to his friends.

"Yeah, just a few minutes will be enough," she quipped. He quickly came near her, placed his hand at her back and guided her towards the lobby. She tried to squirm out of his grasp, but he grabbed her waist tightly. She got the hint that he didn't want to create a scene there, but what surprised her was that she cared. He paced up and she had to scurry a little to keep up. Once they were out of the earshot of people, he pulled her to his front and grumbled, "What the hell are you doing here?"

His brows furrowed and lips formed a tight thin line as if he was gritting his teeth. While preparing to confront him, Reeva had imagined his response in her head, but this was beyond her expectations. Why was he angry? Shouldn't it be otherwise? She tried to understand. She knew that she was growing frail under his fierce stare, so she wrapped herself in her arms and stepped back, putting a little distance between them before replying.

"Yeah, what the hell am I doing here?" she repeated his words, then added, "But why don't you answer first?"—she stressed on the word 'you', placing her index finger on his chest—"What the hell are YOU doing here? Why the hell did you lie to me? Why the hell didn't you tell me about this party? Why the hell didn't you bother to tell me about this place? Why the hell did you introduce me as a friend?" Her voice cracked at the end. She held herself strong and looked straight into his eyes. “What the hell have I done wrong with you? Why the hell are you playing these games with me?”

Agnivesh’s expressions softened as he read the pain in her glossed eyes that she was trying so hard to hide. Taking a step towards her, he opened his arms to embrace her, but she stepped back. “No,” she screamed. “Don’t you dare touch me.”

He stopped at her command, then closed his eyes and raked his hand slowly through his hair. “Okay, let me explain,” he said, his eyes pleading now.

“No. No explanations. You were right. What the hell am I doing here anyway?” She covered her face with her hands. “God! Why the hell am I still talking to you?” She dropped her hands down to her sides and shook her head. “From day one, I knew that this relationship was nothing but just pretence, yet I took a chance. I was so wrong.” She spun on her heel and started pacing down an unfamiliar direction. Agnivesh ran after her and caught her by her arm. As he tried to pull her back, she turned around and slapped him hard. “Damn!” he grimaced. His one hand instantly flew to rub his cheek, while the other remained clenched around her arm.

“Can’t you hear me? Don’t touch me,” she said, trying to wriggle her arm out of his grip, but he swiftly pulled her towards himself, gripped the back of her head with his other hand and locked his lips with hers. She tried to protest in the beginning, but soon gave in. His touch was rough and punishing, yet she felt relaxed as if he was extracting all the wrath out of her with that kiss. ‘*In some relationships, ruining is the only way to fix one another.*’ The words that Agnivesh had said once ricocheted in her head once more. With his lips over hers, she understood the subtext behind those words. He pulled back to look into her eyes, then whispered, “Why are you so stubborn? Can we talk now?”

She nodded and pushed him away slightly. He instantly stepped back, giving her space.

"I am sorry, I lied because I didn't want to hurt you. It wasn't a planned event, and I was so busy that I wouldn't have been able to spend any time with you. That's why I hid it from you."

"This hotel, you own it. Don't you?" she asked, but it came out more like an accusation.

"What do you think this party is for? I bought it just a few days back, and I got it under my name just today." He placed his hands on his hips and looked away in exasperation. "You said you wanted me to get settled here, and I am starting from here," he added, gesturing towards the hotel.

"You didn't bother to invite us here?!"

"Because it wasn't important."

"Yeah, and you introducing me to others as a friend and not as your fiance...I guess, that was not important either," she retorted.

"No. I said so because I am not ready to share the news yet."

"Because suddenly, you are ashamed of my status," she snapped.

"No. I am not ashamed, but are *you* ready? Once I announce this, it's going to be the headline everywhere. Are you ready to handle that?" he asked.

Was she ready? No, she wasn't. How could she announce it to the world when she was ready to blow everything off the moment a doubt popped up in her head? She shook her head and looked down at her clasped hands. "I think you are right, but you could have told me all this before because it's always good to keep a relationship simple, and communication is the only way to achieve that," she tried to make him realize that their relationship was lacking as far as communication was concerned.

“I have learned to deal with relationships in a complicated way. Keeping them simple is too difficult for me. Communication is not my thing, Reeva, and you have to understand that,” he replied. She kept her head down and nodded silently. He exhaled a sigh of relief as if someone had taken weight off his chest. He placed his hands on her shoulders and squeezed them slightly, urging her to look at him. She responded instantly. “Are we okay then?” he asked.

“I think so,” she answered, wriggling her hands. “And I am sorry for the slap,” she added timidly. Agnivesh looked at her for a moment, then said, “You have already slapped me twice. Do it one more time and I am going to punish you hard.”

“It won’t happen again,” she assured.

“Good. Now go home. I will call the driver, he will drop you home,” he said, sliding his hand down his pocket to take out his phone.

“Shit! I can’t go home, I was supposed to attend a meeting, but it’s already too late,” she rambled.

“It’s okay. Come with me. I will drop you there,” he said.

“NO. I have a cab. I will manage myself. Thanks,” she said and took her leave.

Everything went fine that evening. Reeva finalized the deal with the vendor. When she reached home, her mother informed her that they had called Agnivesh for dinner the next day. She was surprised to know that they knew Agnivesh was in town.

“How do you know that he is here?” asked Reeva.

“Prakash called him yesterday regarding fixing the wedding date, and he told us that he is here,” Sumitra shrugged. Reeva had talked to him the day before too, but he hadn't mention anything, neither about being there, nor about the phone call with her father. Did he not tell her because he thought she would pester him to meet? Or had it just slipped out of his mind? Why did she doubt him when she herself had never given him all the details about herself? She closed her eyes and scolded herself for being so skeptical.

"What else did he say?" she asked Sumitra.

"He said that he himself wanted to discuss the wedding date as he has to leave for Singapore for a business meeting next week and wouldn't return for a month, so he wanted to finalize the date as soon as possible so he may clear his schedule for the same," Sumitra said. Why didn't he tell her about his Singapore visit? The question bugged her, but she dismissed it.

The next day, Sumitra and Prakash visited an astrologer to seek all possible auspicious dates for the wedding in the next three months.

Later, Reeva adorned herself for the evening. She wore an off-shoulder navy maxi dress that had long slits at the side. She tied her hair up in a bun on top of her head that accentuated the blue studs she wore in her ears. She highlighted her eyes with a blue eyeliner and wore a dark shade of lipstick as opposed to her usual lip-gloss. She completed the look with striped beige stilettos. It had been ages since she last tried something like that on her. Whenever she planned for her day, the attire would be the last thing on her mind, but not today. Sumitra beamed looking at her daughter.

"Oho! Someone had applied makeup too. Isn't that my lost daughter?" Sumitra said as tears sparkled in her eyes. Reeva blushed feverishly.

"Mumma, I had nothing else to do, so—"

"You don't need to explain anything. I am so happy for you," Sumitra cut her off and caressed her cheek affectionately. The doorbell rang and Reeva turned to open the door. "It must be your father," said Sumitra and resumed her work. She opened the door and was surprised to find that her father wasn't alone; Agnivesh was accompanying him.

"You came early?" Reeva couldn't quell her astonishment as she opened the door.

"I think I am. Shall I go back?" said Agnivesh playfully. Reeva sniggered and shook her head, saying, "No. I didn't mean that. It's just that I wasn't expecting you this early. You always come on time."

Soon, they were all seated and started discussing the wedding dates that the astrologer had suggested. They finalized the first date that was available after Agnivesh's return from Singapore. After dinner, Agnivesh stood up to take his leave, to which Reeva offered to escort him down, and he didn't refuse. She wanted to spend some actual time with him before marriage, but because of his busy schedule, they hardly got any time to themselves. Thus, Reeva didn't want to miss the little tidbits of time she got with him here and there.

"I didn't say it, but I want you to know that you look gorgeous today," Agnivesh said, walking beside Reeva, while their shoulders kept brushing occasionally.

"You won't believe it, but I was actually waiting for you to say that," Reeva said, looking down at her feet. She didn't want him to notice her flushed face. After a hiatus, she looked up at him and said, "We have only forty-seven days before the wedding. Promise me that you will try to spend a little more time with me. I want to know you better before we tie the knot."

He stopped walking and looked back and forth into her eyes for a moment, as if weighing the words he was about to shoot. Reeva instantly felt her stomach dropping.

"What if I say that I am purposely staying away from you," he said, and Reeva gaped in disbelief. She wasn't expecting this. Again, weird thoughts and doubts started swarming her head. "Why?" she asked. He closed the little space between them.

"Do you realize that you are distracting me from my purpose?" he whispered, brushing the back of his fingers over her cheek.

"What purpose?" Her voice was merely a whisper.

"I have been working on something for very long, Reeva. I can't tell you anything right now, but you will come to know it soon. It's crucial for me," he said, dragging his hand back and sliding it into his pocket. Reeva instantly missed his touch.

"If it's so important to you, I won't be your distraction anymore, and I pray for your success," she said.

"What if my success becomes the reason for someone's defeat?" He closed his eyes as if the thought was painful for him.

"No. It can't be. There is only one reason for failure, and that is a lack of effort. One may blame fate too, but the reason can never be someone else's success."

"Sometimes, it's karma too. After all, you reap what you sow."

"Exactly. So don't feel bad and conquer the world," said Reeva, emboldening him like a true partner, but all she could sense on his frowning face was indecisiveness. Why was it so difficult for her to understand this man? She couldn't fathom it. One moment, he seemed ready to hang the moon and stars for her, and the very next moment, he turned aloof and distant. '*Love will fix everything, just give it some time,*' a voice in her head told her. He had fixed her, and now it was her turn to return the favor. She was ready to wait as long as eternity itself to make him realize that she could heal him too. He left with a promise to meet her before he would depart for Singapore.

***

# All About Sona

12 April, 2012

*Dear Diary,*

*Remember, I wrote in yesterday's entry that I feel helpless that I can't express myself to her adequately. Today, Kriti found a solution to that too. She told me that we would converse in written notes. The instant I saw her waiting outside today, I knew that something had happened. The glint in her eyes was missing, and she looked a bit lost. We went to the cafeteria, but unlike other days, she wasn't too interested in talking today. I asked her what had happened, to which she just shook her head. I am so used to her chirpiness that it bothered me to see her so distant and quiet. I wanted to make her feel okay by talking, but I stuttered. She instantly took out a notebook and a pen from her bag and told me to write there. The way she did that should have offended me because she looked irritated, but I don't know why I behave so different when she is around. I picked up that pen and wrote down what was bothering me.*

***What happened? Please tell, and don't say 'nothing' this time.***

*She took the pen from me and wrote:* ***Something came up. I will find the way.***

*I scowled at her and the only thing running in my mind was — Was she making fun of me?*

*"What?" she said aloud, looking at my scowling face. Then, I took the pen from her and wrote:* ***Why are you writing?*** *She looked at the text, snatched the pen from my hand again and started to write, but perhaps she understood what I meant and gave me a sly smile in return. Then, she laughed and said, "God! Why am I writing? I can speak." A smile crept on to my face too.*

*She makes me feel things that I have never felt before. She makes me happy. Then, she started telling me what was bothering her. "You know, we have a DJ night at our college and I have nothing to wear. Everyone is going to wear designer clothes, and I literally have nothing." She paused as the cafeteria guy came to serve us soda lime. "I was so eager for this event. I don't want to miss it. I will have to borrow clothes from Gayatri again and comply with her unreasonable demands in return," she added. I understood what she meant by unreasonable demands. She had been coming here with Gayatri so that she could go on a safe date with her boyfriend. Now I could connect the dots. I took the pen and wrote on the paper:* ***Why don't you buy a new one for yourself?***

*"Because not everyone is born with a silver spoon in their mouth. I can't afford that with my monthly pocket money. I am already running out of money, and asking for more money from dad has never been an option for me," she grimaced.*

***How about I buy you a dress?*** *I wrote on the page.*

*"And why will you do that? What do you want in return? See, if there is anything nasty in your mind, clear it right away. Otherwise, I swear, I won't hesitate breaking your nose," she said angrily, showing me her fist and narrowing her eyes. Didn't I say she is just like me— fierce and dangerous.*

*"No," I spoke and then wrote:* ***I don't want anything in return. Consider it a gift from a friend.***

*She thought a little, then said, "No gifts. But I can consider paying you back in monthly instalments. Is that fine?"*

*I nodded.*

*"Okay, how much do you have?" she asked, straightening her back. I pulled out my wallet from the side pocket, took out a credit card from it and slid it towards her. Her brows rose in surprise. "You have a credit card?" Then, she picked it up and looked at me. "OMG! Your name is embossed on it, Kartik Adiraaj," she said, brushing her fingers over my embossed name. At that moment, I literally felt a tingling on my skin.*

***I have many. Keep it, you may use it whenever you want.*** *I wrote on the page. She looked at me surprisingly and brushed the card against her knuckles. "No doubt, the offer is alluring. But that's gross. How can I keep your card?" she whispered, but the way her voice shook, I knew that she was considering keeping it. However, she slid the card back towards me the very next moment. The dilemma was palpable on her face. Before she could change her mind, I told her in my stuttering voice, "Use it and pay me later." She nibbled on her lip again, then whispered so low that for a moment I thought I had imagined it.*

*"Okay, I will keep it, but the plan has changed now. I will return the money after I get a job, because I am going to buy so many things," she said excitedly. I couldn't help grinning the whole time, thinking that I was the reason behind her smile. I nodded and kept beaming like a lunatic, as if she had agreed to be my girlfriend. But I am hopeful, because now I know that she will definitely be mine one day.*

# 10

The next day, Reeva got a little late for work, as she had gone to the temple with her parents for some puja in the morning. Though they had agreed to give up on that marrying-a-tree thing, they persuaded Reeva to perform another puja instead. She didn't believe in all these things, yet she agreed just because of her parents.

"So, Miss Reeva Panchal, you have a new fan now," Radhika squealed as Reeva walked into the workshop.

"And who is that?" Reeva snickered, dropping her handbag on the table.

"Nitin Gohil, he has been calling incessantly," said Radhika. Reeva tried to recall if she knew anyone by that name. No. She didn't.

"What did he say?" Reeva asked.

"He said that the paintings you created for his friend's office floored him, and now he has a big opportunity for *Kreative Krafts*," Radhika replied.

"Big opportunity?" Reeva asked, astonished.

"Yes. He wants you to organise a party at his house. It's a theme based party, and you are the perfect choice for the job according to him."

"We aren't party planners," Reeva shrugged.

"I told him the same thing, to which he replied that we started with selling paintings, then expanded our business adding other product lines too. Now this is our chance to enter a new market, and I think he has a point."

"Neither do we have the resources, nor the workforce for such an expansion, so all his points are moot. One shouldn't bite off more than one can chew," Reeva said, shaking her head.

"Hmm…I told him that too, and he said we don't need to worry about that. The budget is no issue for him. He just wants you to do it," said Radhika.

Reeva thought about it for a moment, then looked up at Radhika, "What do you suggest?"

"I think we should do it," she said, clasping her hand and bouncing excitedly. Reeva laughed looking at her enthusiasm.

"Can we do it though?" Reeva asked her, nibbling her lip in confusion. More than Radhika, she was asking this of herself.

"Of course we can. All we have to do is Google the right people and outsource everything. As the funds are no issue for him, we can hire the best people in the field for this job. If all goes well, it'll open new doors for us too," she said, then added after a pause, "I feel this is a great opportunity, Reeva. We shouldn't miss it. This is going to be our best bet at this point."

"Okay…I will talk to him about it," she said, stretching the *okay*.

Reeva picked up the office phone and held it in her hand for a while. After preparing herself for the conversation, she dialed his number. He picked up the phone almost immediately, as if he had been waiting for her call. She started discussing the details with him. The guy was persuasive; there was no doubt why Radhika was so excited to work on this project. His offer was undoubtedly tempting, but the only problem was that the party was at night and Reeva was required to stay there for the entire night to organize the event. Reeva also told him that she would need money in advance as she had to make the necessary arrangements, to which he agreed promptly.

The next few days blurred with the pace of light as she busied herself with this new venture she had taken on. After winding up everything quickly, she looked at her watch that displayed quarter to eleven in the morning. She was excited as she was going to meet Agnivesh after almost a week. He had kept his promise and had come to Surat, just to meet Reeva, before he departed for Singapore. Though she didn't discuss it with Agnivesh, she had planned to stay with him for the night and had also taken off from work the next day, so that she might spend the whole thirty-five hours with him before he flew to Singapore. She knew that she wouldn't get a chance to spend time with him afterwards, as the wedding was within a week of his arrival, a month later. In the last few days, she had witnessed a drastic transformation in Agnivesh's demeanor. He had called her every single day and their conversations were not limited to just being about their day. They had talked about their dreams, their future together and so many other silly things as if they were back in their teenage. Picking up her handbag, she blushed thinking about their conversations. When she was about to leave, she saw a white Honda City coming to a halt outside her workshop. A man climbed out of it and ambled towards her.

"Can I meet Ms. Reeva Panchal?" he said as he approached her.

"Yes, I am Reeva Panchal," she replied, studying him top to down.

"Hello ma'am, Nitin sir asked me to deliver you this amount." He took out a bundle of notes wrapped in a black polybag. She had asked for an advance amount, but she wasn't expecting it to be delivered in cash. She cleared her throat and beckoned him to come into her office. Once they were inside, he handed over the amount to her. She took out the money from the envelope and counted the notes. Once the man left her office, she kept the amount inside her handbag and rushed out of the workshop. She was in the cab when her phone buzzed. It was a message from Nitin asking if she had received the amount. She slapped her head, cursing herself that she should have informed him the moment she received the amount. She replied to his message and discussed the other details with him.

Ten minutes later, she was standing outside the hotel where Agnivesh was staying. They had grown very close to each other in the past few days. An intimacy had undoubtedly bloomed between them, despite the distance. She entered the elevator and checked herself in the mirror installed on the wall of the elevator. She had worn a purple button down with blue jeans and the blush on her face perfectly complemented the color of her shirt. She quickly searched for the keycard in her bag when the elevator reached the floor where Agnivesh's room was. She tapped the card on the reader and unlocked the door. As she entered the room, Agnivesh's smiling face greeted her, a face she had recently fallen in love with. Dropping her handbag down, she ran towards him and he took her into a tight embrace. Lifting her up, he twirled her once.

"My girl is here," he said, rubbing his nose against hers, and she giggled in response.

"So, what are the plans for today? I have taken off from work tomorrow and I want you to do the same too. Please," Reeva said, but noticed Agnivesh stiffening in response.

“I am leaving for Singapore tonight, Reeva,” said Agnivesh.

“But you didn’t tell me about the change in your plan,” Reeva’s voice shook imperceptibly.

“Oh! I talked about this with your father, but forgot to inform you. I am sorry,” he answered, raking his hand through his hair.

“It’s okay.” Reeva had made so many plans in her mind, and this sudden alteration disappointed her. “But you were supposed to leave tomorrow night. Why did you prepone it?”

“I needed some time to adjust there before the meeting, so I rescheduled my flight. I didn’t have anything important going here anyway,” he explained, but Reeva’s face clouded with gloom instantly.

“What’s wrong?” asked Agnivesh, reading her expressions.

“We have a wedding planned for the next month and we’ve hardly got any time to spend together, so I had thought of going out for dinner tonight. But it’s okay. Work comes first, I understand.”

He looked at Reeva, then pulled out his mobile from his pocket. He dialed and waited for the person on the other end to pick up the phone. “Can we reschedule my flight to Singapore?” he said over the phone and waited for the response. “Great. Make it for tomorrow then.” He disconnected the phone and looked at Reeva who was beaming at his gesture. She launched herself into his arms elatedly.

“And you are going to stay with me tonight,” he whispered in her ear.

“I already planned for that,” she whispered back. She had lied to her parents that she would be staying at the workshop because of some pending work.

"But there is a problem," Agnivesh said, disengaging himself from her. "I had informed the duty manager here that I would be checking out today," he said and pivoted to call the reception and cancel the checkout, but they informed him that they had already allotted the room to someone else.

"What will we do now?" Reeva asked as soon as he disconnected the phone.

"How about going to my hotel?" Agnivesh suggested, but Reeva's expressions darkened as if she had seen a ghost. *The Grand Rajvilaas.* How could she forget that hotel? It was the place that had changed her life forever. "No," she said instantly, and her voice came out a little louder than she had intended.

"Okay, relax. We won't go there. Let me call Manish. He will look for another hotel," he said and called Manish at the same time. She couldn't hear any of his conversation with Manish, as there was too much noise within her. How was she going to explain her reaction at the mention of that hotel? She was sure that it hadn't gone unnoticed by Agnivesh.

"It's just too far, so I didn't want to go there," she started explaining as she saw him approaching her.

"It's okay. You said 'no', and that's perfectly fine," he said smiling.

Soon, they checked out and headed towards the other hotel that Manish had booked for them. Reeva didn't find the new hotel as good as the previous one, but she was more concerned about spending time with him, rather than fuss about the hotel. They settled in their allotted room and ordered lunch. Everything was going fine, but as time passed, Reeva observed a change in Agnivesh's demeanor. He looked nonchalant and distant again that made Reeva wonder where things had gone wrong! She played their entire conversation in her mind since they had met that day, but couldn't come up with anything that could have hurt him. Maybe it was the pressure of business, she conjectured. At night, Reeva couldn't stop herself from asking him when she saw him getting ready. "What's wrong? Are you going somewhere?"

"Something came up and I need to go. You stay here and order dinner for yourself," he said, buttoning his cufflinks. Reeva noticed he didn't look at her when he said that.

"What about you?" she asked.

"I may come in late, don't bother to wait up for me," he replied, again looking at the door.

"But you said—" Reeva started, but he stopped her, holding a hand up.

"Reeva, a few things aren't in my hands. I had cleared this thing in the beginning itself that business will always be my priority."

"Yes, I remember," Reeva said forlornly. He had told her this in the beginning, but they didn't share a relationship then. Even she had assumed that her business would be her priority over everything, but she had started considering him above anything else now. Why couldn't he do the same for her? Was it wrong to change priorities as a relationship grew? she thought. Leaving her engrossed in her own thoughts, Agnivesh left the room, slamming the door behind him.

It was quarter to twelve at night when Agnivesh returned to the room. She was still awake and had tried to call him many times, but there was no network in the hotel. She was angry with him, but kept her composure.

"You haven't slept?" He was surprised to see her awake. Reeva noticed his slurred speech.

"You are drunk." It wasn't a question, as it hadn't taken Reeva much time to realize that he was drunk.

"Yeah, I told you I had a meeting," he said, looking out the window, unable to meet her eyes.

"What do I mean to you, Agnivesh?" she poured out her heart.

"What kind of a question is this?" he said, unbuttoning his shirt.

"If one day, you have to choose between me and your business, what will you choose?" she asked and squeezed her eyes shut, realizing that she was expecting too much. Agnivesh kept looking at her flummoxed. She opened her eyes, her heart sped up and her stomach sank as the next few words rolled over her tongue.

"I love you, Agnivesh," she whispered, and a solemn tear rolled down her cheek. He looked at her with his brows rutted in confusion. These weren't the words he was expecting from her. His hand flew instantly to his head as he pressed his temples and then raked his hand through his hair in exasperation.

"I have fallen in love with you, Agnivesh. I have started to envision us as a family. And when you distance yourself like this, it hurts me," she said. Agnivesh shook his head slightly, looking at her despondently.

She took a step ahead and closed the distance between them. "I love you," she repeated, holding his face in her trembling hands.

"Don't say that. Not now. Not ever. I don't deserve your love. I am going to break you into pieces. You should stay far away from me," he said with despair in his eyes, but Reeva's reaction surprised him again.

She laughed.

"Remember, I said the same thing once? And do you remember what you had said then? That in some relationships, ruining each other is the only way to fix one another. I believed your words then, and now they have become my hope. Our relationship is going to be one of those kind. And

I am ready for it," she said, raising herself up and pulling his head slightly down. She locked her lips with his in a kiss. He hesitated in the beginning, but soon gave in and returned the kiss with the same passion, as if there was no tomorrow. Reeva bloomed at his touch, but then suddenly he pulled back and pushed her away slightly. "We need to stop, otherwise I may cross the boundaries," he said, catching his breath.

"Let's not draw any boundaries tonight. Let's get lost in each other and see if it ruins or heals when two broken hearts meet," she whispered against his lips and took him again in a kiss. She poured all her emotions and pent-up longing into that kiss and let him get immersed in the essence of her love. The possibility of getting healed through love is worth every fight, and she was determined to fix both of them with her belief in her love. The way he held her made her realize that he too believed in it, but was adamant to admit it. But he didn't hold back this time. He lifted her up in his arms and took her to the bed.

They explored not just each other's bodies, but souls too, letting their vulnerable sides be exposed to each other. His touch felt smooth, comforting and healing, even though it had a gist of roughness to it. Reeva smiled to herself as a tear peeped over the corner of her eye, thinking how far they had come in their relationship. Until a few weeks back, she had wanted to run away from him as far as possible, but today, she was not only prepared but also desperate to imbue herself thoroughly in his color. He didn't disappoint her either as he blended her in his hue all the way by sinking deep inside her, and touching her soul and beyond. That very moment, she realized that she was irrevocably in love with him. Her relationship with Agnivesh still had many layers yet to be unveiled. Nevertheless, it felt soul-deep.

It was around three in the morning when Reeva's eyes flickered open because of some clank in the room. She got up and saw Agnivesh sitting on the edge of the couch perched in one corner of the room. He had rested his elbows on his knees and held his head in his hands. She looked down at the floor where a glass was still rolling back and forth. She understood that he had been drinking again. What was wrong with him? Why was he behaving that way all of a sudden? she asked herself, but had no answer.

"What happened?" she asked, bolting upright and covering herself with a white sheet.

"We did a mistake, Reeva," he answered, staying in the same position. Reeva winced at his choice of words.

"No, we didn't. Don't insult us by calling it a mistake. We love each other, and that reason is enough—" She stopped midway suddenly as the realization hit her that he had never confessed that he loved her, but this wasn't the right time to bring that up.

"Is there anything else bugging you?" she asked, sitting beside him. He paused for a moment and looked blankly into the distance. Then, he rubbed his face with his hands.

"I am going to do something, Reeva, but I am not sure if I should do it." He looked up at her.

"Will it give you your peace of mind?" she asked.

"I think so," he said, then shook his head. "I don't know."

"Then do it. You will never know until you do it, and even if it turns out to be a bad move, at least you will learn a lesson for life. But if you don't do it now, it will keep tormenting you forever," she said and brushed his hair back with her fingers.

"What happened then, Reeva?" he said out of nowhere, grabbing her hand and looking straight into her eyes.

"When?" she whispered, holding her breath, dreading where the conversation was going with this question.

"Forget it," he said, waving his hand. "Just tell me, do you regret anything that you have done in your past?" he asked, and the question had more weight to it. Did she regret anything? She introspected for a moment, but couldn't answer.

"Just answer in a *yes* or *no*," said Agnivesh, making it easier for her.

"No. I don't regret anything. I believe that one should never regret the decisions made in the past, because that might be the best thing one could do at that time, keeping that situation and the time in mind. The outcome is not what we expect sometimes, but that doesn't mean our actions were wrong." Anguish glistened in her eyes. She was certainly disappointed with the outcome, but not with her actions, and even if a part of her regretted, she wasn't going to admit it aloud. She knew that once she would voice her remorse, it would become real and her own conscience would kill her. She was just saving herself.

They say one should leave the past behind and live in the present to build a better future. But is it that easy? Sometimes, the present is deeply rooted in the past. You live in it with every breath you take. Every single action you take or thought you have is the consequence of that one moment in the past. She looked up at him and found him staring at her with his brows knitted in confusion...or perhaps, displeasure. She dismissed the conversation by walking away from him and slid back into her comforter. She wasn't ready to share anything else with him, and felt that perhaps she would never be able to. Some secrets should die with you because once they are out, they do nothing good except destroy the present.

***

## All About Sona

13 April, 2012

*Dear Diary,*

*Why are people such jerks? Why do they stare at a girl as if she is on display for them and they have the right to do that? And why are a few girls so stupid that they ignore it instead of reacting? Today, something happened. When we were heading towards the cafeteria, I saw a few guys staring at Sona. I know I shouldn't blame her dress, which was too tight and clinging to her body in a way that all her curves were on display, because it's not about the clothes but the mindset, but still, why to wear anything too attention seeking and make yourself a center-piece? I didn't say this to her, but I did glower at those jerks. It wouldn't have surprised me at all if she had smashed the face of one of those guys, but instead, she ignored it. Perhaps because one of them was Raunak. Her crush. I glared back, especially at him, and softly kept my hand at the small of her back to let them know that I was with her. She instantly looked at me as she felt my touch, then rose up on her tippy toes to whisper in my ear, "I know what you are doing. Keep your hands to yourself, or I won't mind breaking them."*

*I looked back at her, flabbergasted. Was I doing anything wrong?*

*"What?" I asked, surprised at her jibe.*

*"You are trying to show people that I am your girlfriend," she seethed. Was I doing that? Perhaps yes, because I wanted that guy to know that she was off-limit.*

*"But I am not. Don't forget that ever," she added, hauling me out of my trance.*

*"I know," I answered. Then suddenly, she came to my side and slid her hand in mine.*

*"But now, I can call you my close friend," she whispered, and all kinds of emotions crossed my mind. I was elated. Astounded. And anxious. She held my hand and hauled me into the cafeteria.*

*"You know, I shopped using your credit card yesterday," she said, pulling a chair to sit on.*

*"And the amount was huge"—she stretched her arms to indicate 'huge'—"I hope you won't mind," she added. I knew the amount. I had received a message the moment she made the payment, and it was just four thousand something.*

*"I won't," I answered.*

*"Hmm...anyway, just a few thousand aren't going to burn a hole in your father's pocket, and I will definitely return it after getting a job."*

*We sat there for about an hour. She showed me pictures of the dresses that she had bought online using my card. Yes, my card; I say it again and again because it makes me feel like I am a part of her life.*

*Then, I took her for a drive in my black Porsche, and she was so elated the whole time. The Porsche used to be my first love, but after Sona, it has descended to the second position. I don't understand why I feel so deeply connected to her? I have read somewhere that this is nothing but infatuation, just a physical attraction. A sudden surge of serotonin, a hormone that causes the feeling of being in love. It's just a chemical cause. There is nothing emotional in it. Is it the same with me? Do I feel just physically attracted to Sona? No. Instead, I want to connect with her emotionally. Just the realization that she is near gives me the feeling of heaven. I can spend my entire life only looking at her and listening to her. Does that mean my love is pure and eternal? They say, true love never goes unnoticed. Does she see it when she looks into my eyes? I have no answer to it, and I don't want one either. The thought that my love may remain unrequited scares me to hell. So even if it's an illusion, I am going to make it my home. I don't know what will happen tomorrow, but today I am happy, and I have her as a close friend.*

# 11

*I look down from the terrace of the hotel — The Grand Rajvilaas, and suddenly feel as if someone has dragged the ground beneath my feet. I am scared of heights, it always makes me dizzy. I instantly pivot and heave a sigh of relief. I take only a few steps ahead when I hear a scream. It's a female voice and I know this voice by heart, but it stifles so instantly that I wonder if I am hallucinating. I turn my head towards the direction of the sound and start walking. I can still hear the muffled sound of struggle, so I start taking longer strides. As soon as I reach there, I see something that scares me out of my wits. I see him lying over a girl. A girl I know so well. The girl I have always struggled to be like. But today, she is in trouble and needs my help. I know that if I don't act quickly, she may lose her life. The boy has pinned her to the ground by holding both her hands above her head, while his other hand has covered her mouth to muffle her screams. Gloom and fear slide into my heart, threatening to choke me. The sight is frightening. Though he has trapped that girl, it's I who is getting smothered. The girl is looking at me for help, and I want to help her too, but I can't move. I feel like my feet have turned into stone. I try to scream for help, but words fail to spurt out of my mouth. I try to run and call someone for help, but I'm immobile. The girl is dying in front of me, but I am unable to do anything for her. Then, the girl stops fighting. Her eyes are still open, but the life in them is gone. She is dead. The girl who used to be so effervescent and full of life at one time is now lying lifeless there. Suddenly, I get my voice back and I scream, putting my whole energy into it, but it is of no use now.*

*Instead, it attracts the attention of that boy, and he looks at me. Panic gushes into my heart and twists my gut. He starts walking towards me with gradual steps. I have ample time to run and save my life, but I am frozen there. His face is surging with rage, his hands clenched at his sides and his eyes red. Once his proximity disturbs my balance, I start running in no particular direction to keep myself away from him. Having nowhere to go, I run to the barricade of the terrace and cling to it as if it would save me. He is still approaching me at the same pace. My mind is frozen and my senses numb. I don't know what I'll do next. When he comes near me, I gather all the courage I have and grab his collar. I push him hard, and I don't know how it happens, but the next moment I see him falling down from the 15th floor of the building. Unable to do anything else, I start yelling, 'I didn't push you. I didn't kill you,' while he slowly disappears into the abyss. And then, there is a loud bang.*

Reeva jolted and her eyes flickered open. She looked around frantically. Taking in the view of the hotel room, she realized that she was having the same nightmare again. Her heart was thumping in her chest as if it were about to explode, and her whole body was drenched in sweat. She heard the loud bang again and realized it was coming from the door. She covered herself with the white sheet on the bed and was about to gather her clothes when the door swung open. Before she could understand what was happening, two women constables entered the room and took her into custody. Before she could find out where Agnivesh was, she was thrown into the police van along with thirteen other girls.

Before she realized that she had to cover her face just like the other girls, the media clicked her. Everything happened so fast that she had to bite her tongue repeatedly to assure herself that she wasn't in a dream still. But no, everything was indeed happening for real. She had mistakenly been caught in some sex racket going on at the hotel. Her phone and her bag were in police custody separately, so she couldn't even call anyone.

"Please let me make just one call. I am not the kind of girl you presume me to be," she requested the lady cop, adjusting her clothes that she had put on in haste. She was at the police station now, standing in front of the police officer's table, while the other girls sat quietly on benches perched at the end of the room.

"You think I am a fool? I have seen hundreds of such cases in my career, and I know well whom to believe and not. Now go and sit there quietly, just like the other girls," she reprimanded Reeva.

"Ma'am, please try to understand. I was there with my fiancee and I can prove it, just let me make a call," she elucidated. Suddenly, one of the girls got up and came near them.

"She is right, ma'am. We aren't that kind of girls. She was there with her fiancee, and I was there with my husband," the girl said dramatically, then showed them the black beaded necklace around her neck. "See, I am wearing my *mangalsutra* too," she added.

Reeva closed her eyes with the realization that there was no way she could prove herself innocent. "Ma'am, just one call. Please," she tried one more time.

"Shut up, just shut your mouth up. Otherwise, you will be the first to go behind bars," yelled the police officer. The other girl returned to her seat instantly, while Reeva kept looking at the officer for help. "Didn't you hear what

I said?" the police officer yelled again, and Reeva turned back. Instead of sitting on the bench with the other girls, she chose to lean against the wall.

What was happening with her, and where the hell was Agnivesh? She closed her eyes, thinking about the predicament she was in.

About an hour later, Reeva saw her parents entering the police station. She was about to rush to them when one of the lady cops held her hand up and gestured at her to stay where she was. She saw her parents going into the SHO's office. From the distance, she could see them nodding to something that the SHO was saying, though she couldn't hear any of it. The SHO showed them her bag and her phone. She wondered about its contents; what could be in there to show them! Both of them sat there for a while and filled some form. After a few minutes, they came towards Reeva, and the lady cop allowed her to leave with them. Once they were out of the police station, Reeva started to explain, but Prakash held his hand up and gestured at her to not say anything. The look he gave Reeva was full of disgust and shame. Reeva instantly felt a sting in her heart.

"What does this look mean? Do you believe what they told you at the police station?" she asked.

"Let's not talk about it here. You have already insulted us enough. Don't create a scene now. Moreover, there is no reason to doubt them," her father said, looking away from her.

"Now I understand why you used to run from home every other day. This is what you have been doing, while we thought you were working hard at your so-called workshop," Sumitra, her mother, seethed through her gritted teeth.

"So you think that low of me," Reeva said, darting her gaze from her father to her mother. She couldn't believe that her own parents were doing this to her.

"First of all, what were you doing at that cheap hotel? That too after you lied at home that you would be staying at the workshop," Prakash asked.

"I was with Agnivesh there," Reeva replied, and it sounded like a white lie even to her own ears. Sumitra threw her hands up in the air.

"Do you think we are fools? Why would Agnivesh go to that hotel when he has his own hotel in the city?" Sumitra asked. Prakash held Sumitra's hand and urged her, "Please, let's not talk here. People are watching."

"No. We have to talk about it right here, right now," Reeva said obstinately.

"Okay. As you wish. Stop fooling us with your lies, Reeva. We know that Agnivesh is already out of the country. He left for Singapore last night, then how could he have been with you last night?" Prakash hissed.

"He was. Just call him and ask him once. He rescheduled his flight so that he could spend some time with me. Just ask him once," Reeva answered.

"And what about this?" Sumitra asked, opening Reeva's handbag and showing her the cash that she had kept in it the previous day.

"It's the booking amount from one of my clients," she said, but the words felt odd on her tongue. Why would one pay such a hefty amount to someone who had just started her business? "I know how it looks, but trust me, it is from a client," Reeva added.

"This client?" Her father opened a chat on her mobile and showed it to her. It was the same chat that she had had the previous day with Nitin Gohil.

"Yes, that's him," she said while going through the chat that read:

**Nitin: Ma'am, have you received the money?**

**Reeva: Yes.**

**Nitin: Let me remind you, I need you for the full night.**

**Reeva: Yes, I remember that. But I will stay only till five in the morning.**

**Nitin: That's ok with me. I'll pay more if you want, but I really need you.**

**Reeva: The amount is enough for now, will let you know if I need more.**

**Nitin: Thank you so much for accepting my proposal.**

**Reeva: My pleasure.**

And with that, she understood that all the signs were against her. Still, they were her parents and if they didn't believe her, how could she prove herself innocent in front of others.

"Oh, God! It's not what it looks like," she said, but her father cut her off. "Enough, Reeva. It's in the news too. Stop creating a scene here and come with us."

"I am not coming," Reeva said. "If you don't trust me, I can't stay at your place anymore," she added.

"Then go wherever you want to go, but keep one thing in mind, if anything like this happens again, don't bother calling us. Consider your parents dead from now on," her father said and left Reeva there alone.

Time is no one's friend. You never know when it turns in your favor or against you. Till the day before, she felt like her life was coming back on track. Little did she know that it was only taking a U-turn. She tried to reach Agnivesh on his number, but it was switched off. Having nowhere to go, she headed towards her workshop. She was still wearing her clothes from the previous day. When she reached there, she was surprised to see the workshop closed. She looked at the time; it was already quarter to one in the afternoon. She opened the workshop with her set of keys and instantly started calling her staff over the phone, so that she may begin the work. She opened her handbag for her phone, and the bundle of cash in that pocket stared back at her. She had thought that this amount would help her take her business to a new level; little did she know that it was going to finish everything for her. She typed a message and sent it to all five of her employees. She waited for some time, and when no response came from anyone even after two hours, she called up Radhika. She picked up the call instantly.

"Did you get my message? It's already 2:30, when are you coming?" Reeva asked, twisting her wrist to confirm the time.

"Oh! I didn't check. I thought the workshop would remain closed today. Actually, we saw you on the news only this morning—" she stopped mid-sentence, and Reeva understood what she meant.

"Are you coming?" Reeva asked.

"No Reeva, my father says I should stay at home for now, so I won't be able to come. You may look for my replacement," she replied.

"Is it because of the news?" Reeva asked.

"Umm…Reeva…I need to go. Bye." She terminated the call abruptly.

Reeva held her head in her hands. Everything was slipping out of her hands right in front of her eyes and she was unable to do anything. Her own people had turned their backs on her in the hour of need, while the only person whom she could count on was out of the picture all of a sudden. Her eyes burned with unshed tears. The last few hours of her life had been an ordeal, yet she hadn't let a single tear fall. This is the thing about pain; we might think that it's making us hollow from the inside, but in reality, it makes us strong like a rock. Either that, or she had turned herself into stone, not letting anything affect her anymore. She had seen worse than this before. If she could bear that pain, this was nothing in comparison. She untied her hair and massaged her head lightly with her fingertips. A headache that she had been ignoring all this while started to make its presence felt now. She tied her hair up again and started to work on the pending projects. '*If I could start this business all alone, I can take it further all alone too*. I can do it. I will do it,' she muttered to herself. Giving up had never been an option for her. She believed that one wins half the battle already when one decides to try, and moreover, giving up would not only kill her dreams, but her too.

She was engrossed in work when she heard a bustle at the entrance. She looked up and saw Raghu, one of her workers, entering. "Why are you here?" she asked.

"For work. You messaged me to come here. My daughter wasn't well, so I got late," he replied. She smiled softly, thinking that perhaps he hadn't seen the news yet. "Didn't you see the news?" she asked him, looking down at the ground.

"I have, Didi. But I know that's all a lie. These news channels just need *masala* and show anything. I know you, and I know that you won't ever do anything like that," he said, keeping his bag in the almirah. With that, the first tear rolled down Reeva's cheek. She had stood like a rock when the whole world seemed to stand against her, and now when she finally got a little support, she started melting like wax.

"Don't cry, Didi. No one is going to believe it. You are such a kind-hearted person, even God will think twice before doing anything bad to you. I can't even imagine what would have happened to my family had you not offered me this job," he said, picking up the boxes of packed articles.

“Everyone believes it, Raghu. No one is coming back to work here,” she sobbed silently.

“That’s even better, Didi. They were all slackers anyway. We will hire better people,” he tried to joke, and Reeva smiled.

“We have so much work and so little time. How are we going to do this?” she asked, more to herself than him. She knew that Raghu was unskilled for the job. He used to do all the labor work around the workshop. He was destitute when she had found him begging on the street. He was much younger than her, and had a wife, a sister and a kid to look after. They had come from some village in Bihar after losing their land because of some loan his father couldn’t pay back. She had offered him this job, and he put his heart and soul into it.

“Didi, till the time you don’t get any new employees, I will call my wife and sister to come help you. They aren’t very good at all this, but they will learn,” he suggested. Reeva instantly approved his suggestion, not that she had any option.

***

# All About Sona

14 April, 2012

*Dear Diary,*

*My hand is bleeding and aching while I am writing this today. Can you believe it? I had sworn I would never show this side of me to Sona, yet I scared her today. But she is an angel. She surprised me today. Despite being scared, she calmed me down. She fought for me, holding my hand in hers all this while. Let me tell you from the beginning:*

*As usual, we were sitting in the cafeteria when a group of boys came in. I ignored them because I knew who they were. I had fought with them once before when they damaged my Porsche. I gestured to Sona to get up and leave the place, and she understood. But when we were getting up, one of them made a crude remark at Sona, and I instantly glared at him. "Why are you looking at me that way? She isn't your car," one of the boys said. I ignored it and kept walking, keeping my hand on Sona's back.*

*"Hey, just sit down. He won't speak because he knows that once he starts, he won't be able to finish." They all laughed.*

*I tightened my fists and bit my tongue to keep my anger in control.*

*"And the girl would run," another one added, and they all started laughing even harder.*

*"B-b-b-b-b-b...baby, c-c-c-c—" someone tried to mimic me, but one of them cut him off. "Please stop it, yaar. I think the girl is more interested in a talk-less relationship."*

*We were at the exit door when I heard this and blood rushed in my veins. I stopped there instantly, but Sona held my arm this time and dragged me out. Once we were out, I yanked her hand away forcefully and made her stumble. I needed to take out the wrath that was surging inside me. I punched the wall so hard that my knuckles started bleeding right away. I heard Sona gasp, then saw her rushing towards me and trying to hold my hand, but I pushed her away and punched one more time. This time, it was the window's glass. It shattered instantaneously, leaving my hand covered in blood.*

*"Please, don't do it. Stop it," I heard her say, and turned to look at her. She was scared, so scared that it felt like she would start crying any moment. She came near me, taking each step warily. Once she was in front of me, she held both of my hands in hers and told me timorously, "Close your eyes." I kept looking at her astounded. What was she trying to do? She raised her hand up and kept it over my eyes. "Close your eyes," she whispered again. "Now think about the person you love the most and count till ten," she added.*

*Did I really need to close my eyes to see the person I loved the most when she was standing in the flesh right in front of me? I followed her command anyway. I didn't want to scare her any more than I already had. When I opened my eyes again, she asked, "Feeling better?" and I nodded in response.*

*"Good, now come with me," she said and dragged me back into the cafeteria, holding my uninjured hand in hers. I stopped her by pulling her hand. She turned towards me and asked, "Do you trust me?" and I nodded. "Then come with me and promise me you won't leave my hand, no matter how much they provoke you. Okay?" She looked at me for a response, and I nodded again.*

*She held my hand tightly when we padded towards that group. They all looked at us and started laughing again.*

*"Laugh. Laugh as much as you can. But for once, just look at his hand"—she pointed first towards my bleeding hand and then towards the broken glass— "and also that*

*window. Now thank him that he didn't do this to your faces. Imagine what would have happened to you if he hadn't controlled his anger," she said, while the boys didn't give a shit about all that she said.*

*"Oh! She is here to do the talking on his behalf," one of the boys told his mates and then pointed towards Sona. "Now imagine what would happen to him when we complain about this damage," he said, and Sona just shrugged.*

*"What will happen? Maybe the authorities will tell him to be careful next time, or maybe they will be more worried about his bleeding hand. After all, his father owns this college," she said, and all the boys looked at each other. I looked at her astounded. How did she know that?*

*"And let me tell you one more thing. Do you know he was expelled from his previous college just because he smashed some guy's face and that guy is still roaming with his disfigured face. So if you don't want that to happen to you as well, please keep your tongues locked in your mouth," she added. Without giving them another chance to speak, she stormed out, dragging me behind her. She knows everything about me, while I was scared that she would run away if she ever came to know the truth about my temperament. How wrong was I? I have never told her anything, then how did she know? I was confused, but later when I asked her about this, she told me everything.*

*"Gayatri told me all about you," she said, but I kept looking at her for more. She understood and continued, "Her boyfriend talked to her about you, and she warned me to stay away from you." I felt annoyed and elated at the same time. Annoyed, because how dare she tell Sona to stay away from me, and elated because Sona didn't heed her warning anyway. I asked her why she had disregarded her friend's advice? I needed to know why she believed me over her friend.*

*"Because she doesn't know you and I do," she replied with a shrug, and my eyes glistened with pride. I feel as if I have finally got my voice back. She is my voice and she believes me. I had the urge to touch her and hold her close to my heart. I wanted her to listen to my heartbeat and know how precious she is for me. I wanted to hide her in me, away from the world, so that no one could ever tell her to stay away from me. But I couldn't do any of that. She hasn't given me that right yet. At that moment, looking into her eyes, I promised myself that I would never let her smile fade away, I would kill myself to fulfil all her desires, I would never let her walk away from me, even if she wants to.*

~

# 12

Almost a month had passed since that incident at the hotel. Even though Reeva had somehow managed to go through the ordeal, it still stung her heart that Agnivesh never tried to contact her after that day. The news was all over television, media and the newspapers, but it soon got buried under the other happenings around the city. The best (as well as the worst) thing about today's world is that people are so busy and there is such an overload of information with so many incidents happening everyday that they forget about incidents almost as quickly as they first react to it. The same thing happened in her case too. People reacted, she lost her employees as well as some of her deals in the beginning, but her life slowly started to come back on track. Raghu was the first one to support her, then two others returned to work after a few days. She hadn't spoken to her parents since that incident, neither had they tried to contact her. The one person whose number she kept dialing frequently though was Agnivesh, but she couldn't reach him. She had also spoken to Manish, Agnivesh's PA, and came to know from him that Agnivesh had to leave for Singapore early that morning. Even he hadn't been in touch with him since. She was angry with him, but also concerned. He had been worried about something the night before that incident had happened.

Agnivesh was the only person who could prove her innocence to her parents, because he knew that she was with him that night. Her heart sank thinking that he might have seen the news and was now scared of accepting her as his fiancee in front of people. A meek voice in her head told her that he wouldn't ever return to her. She shook her head to clear the thought. *It's always good to look forward because if you keep looking back, even a pebble in your path will get the power to topple you down.* She reminded herself of her mantra before entering the hotel where she was going to display her products for the first time at the Expo organized by REM Ltd.

Dressed in a raw silk saree with her hair pinned up in a neat bun, she gazed at the lavish entrance of the hotel that was decorated exquisitely for the ongoing event. She walked over to her stall in the exhibition hall where two of her artisans had already started displaying their best products. The event started and the venue overflowed with the elite of the city. *Kreative Krafts*' stall was able to catch the attention of the crowd as their products were unique in design and were made with eco-friendly material. She was happy with the response they were getting, but her eyes kept searching for Agnivesh in the crowd. Didn't he tell her that he was a major sponsor of the event? She kept looking for him with the hope that he must be present there, but with no luck. She started packing things up as the closing time approached.

Suddenly then, a male figure caught Reeva's attention. She quickly told her workers to wind up the stall, and rushed after him. It didn't take her much to recognize who it was. She had expected him to be there, but not that he would give her the cold shoulder. All the qualms and fears that she had in her mind were turning out to be real, and she was eager to confront them. Jostling and weaving through the crowd, she saw him entering a room that seemed like an office. She rushed towards it, but was stopped at the door by a man dressed in the hotel staff's uniform.

"Ma'am, it's the meeting room," he said.

"I need to meet Mr. Agnivesh Solanki. It's urgent."

"Ma'am, we are strictly instructed not to disturb them. You can take an appointment for later and meet him."

"Can you please just inform him once that I am waiting for him outside? My name is Reeva Panchal. He knows me well," she pleaded.

"Just a minute," he said, considering her plea, and disappeared into the room. Only a beat had passed when he returned. "Ma'am, he says he doesn't know you," he said.

Reeva gasped and her ears reddened in embarrassment. Why was she so surprised? Didn't she already know that he was ignoring her? He knew that she would be there for the event, yet he didn't care to talk to her. And now, he had even refused to recognize her. Mortified, she just smiled at him and turned around. The whole way back, she chided herself for having expected too much of him. She felt angry and betrayed. She reached her workshop and unlocked it. Since that fateful day, she had made her workplace her home. Her parents had already assumed that Agnivesh would never marry her, but she had had a meek hope that he would perhaps come back to her as he alone knew the truth, but that hope also got shattered that day. 'I have seen the worst, and if I could get through that, I will get through this too,' she whispered to herself while unlocking her workshop. She kept tossing and turning in bed the whole night. It was quarter to three in the morning when her phone buzzed with a message. When she checked it, she bolted upright in her bed. It was a text from Agnivesh, that read: **Meet me today at the hotel The Grand Rajvilaas at 5 AM.**

Why did he want to meet her that early in the morning? The first question popped up in her mind. That too at the hotel she was so uncomfortable with? Popped question two. Why had he messaged her at this odd hour? Had he been unable to sleep too after the way he behaved with her? And then popped another. She was so lost in these questions that kept popping in her mind that she didn't even realize how an hour passed. Soon, she was in a cab heading towards the hotel. She reached the hotel five minutes before time. Her phone buzzed in her hand as soon as she alighted from the car. It was another message from Agnivesh.

**Take the elevator and come straight to the terrace.**

She clenched the phone tightly in her hand as she read the message. She looked up at the fifteen-floor high building of *The Grand Rajvilaas*. An instant nostalgia gushed through her heart and she felt too dizzy to take a step ahead. She turned around and slid back inside the cab. 'I can't do this,' she thought, without realizing that she was also saying it out loud.

"Ma'am, shall I take you back?" the cab driver asked. Her heart pleaded with her to go back. She wanted to run away from this place, but a voice in her head told her to stay and meet him. The confrontation with truth may torment you for a moment, but running away from it will keep you in despair forever. She wanted to put an end to all this, so she stepped out of the cab and headed towards the entrance. She took the elevator. With every count going up on the display screen of the elevator, she felt her heart drowning deeper into the inferno. As the elevator stopped, her heartbeat came to a stop too. As she climbed up the same set of stairs that she had taken four years back, memories of that day started flashing in front of her eyes. The terrace door was open, just like it had been that day. Anxiety roiled in her gut as she saw Agnivesh standing near the barricade with his back turned towards her. She cautiously took each step towards him. Her instincts were telling her incessantly that this day was going to reshuffle everything in her life. Perhaps it would break her again and in so many pieces this time that it wouldn't be easy for her to gather them back together. Instead of turning back, however, she went ahead to test her boundaries.

"Good morning, Reeva." Agnivesh sensed her presence and turned towards her with an unapologetic smile on his face, as if nothing had happened.

"I don't understand all this," she stuttered.

"You don't need to. See, I am here for you now," he said with the same smile still plastered on his face, but his taut jaw revealed his annoyance. Reeva closed her eyes momentarily to pull herself together. Perhaps, she was overthinking.

"Yesterday—" Reeva started to say, but he cut her off. "I have my limitations, Reeva. I can't always act the way you want me to," he said, taking her in his arms and Reeva let him. With that one hug, Reeva realized how much she had craved for it.

"Why did you leave me alone that day? You have no idea what I had to through," Reeva sobbed silently, melting in his arms.

"I had to, Reeva. I told you, I had an important meeting to attend," he said, and Reeva nodded in response. After a pause, he added, "Moreover, I wanted you to realize how it feels when the person you trust the most leaves you in your toughest times."

His words could have soothed the pain she had endured over the past few weeks, but they didn't. The hiss in his voice and the hidden accusation in his words irked her. His cryptic words were infused with rage. She looked up at him with her moist eyes and witnessed for the first time an emotion on his face that was unknown to her. It was a sentiment laced with hatred, pure hatred that twisted like a dagger in her chest, and…perhaps, pain too.

It was some pain that she had caused him, but through all the hate in his eyes, could he see the pain that he had given her? She instantly wriggled out of his embrace and took a step back.

"Why do you sound so different?" she asked. He smiled at her again and took a step ahead. Holding her shoulders with his hands, he said, "No one is real in this world, Reeva. Everything is either an illusion or pretence. We all are wearing masks and sometimes, we become so habitual of this mask that we forget our real identity." Reeva instantly looked at her left shoulder. Agnivesh clenched it tightly and the car keys that he had been holding in his hand pricked into her skin. However, his words hurt her more than any physical pain. When she looked up at him again, she found him staring back at her, as if trying to read something.

"And today, I am here to remind you who you are... *Sona*."

With that one word, her whole universe tilted around her. She instantly yanked his hands off of her shoulders and took a step back. "Who are you?" The words immediately spurted out of her mouth, as if she was meeting him for the first time.

"*Karma*–it's the strongest force in the whole universe. You can change your name, your identity, your address, but it doesn't care for all that to come back to you." He lifted his right hand up and the keys—that she had recognized as his car's—hung on his index finger. "Do you know what happens when you make someone fall in love with you, show them new heights"—he lifted his hand up a little and Reeva's eyes followed the keys hanging by his fingers—"and when you are done with them, you drop them down?" He dropped the car keys and Reeva gasped, hearing the sound that the keys made upon hitting the ground. Reeva kept looking at that set of keys with her eyes wide open. "Did you do this to *him*, Sona?"

Reeva looked at him astonished.

"Why did you do that to *him*? Why did you do that to me?" he asked, and she saw a twinge of pain spreading across his face. What had she done to him? She tried to recall. She hadn't even been aware of his existence in the world before the day he came to her parents with a marriage proposal, but he certainly had done wrong to her. A familiar pain sprang up in her chest, but she pushed it back down as he was yet to answer why he had done that to her.

"Why am I not surprised to think that whatever happened a few weeks back was all planned by you? You know that I was with you, that I am innocent, don't you? Yet, you never came forward. You let people talk ill about me."

"See, now you understand everything. How could I have done that?" he said, looking away from her, then locking his gaze back with hers. "It wasn't in the plan," he added.

"Plan?" she laughed humorlessly, while tears started to pool in her eyes. "Why did you need a plan to break me? What wrong had I done to you?"

"Do you really want to know?" he asked, then took out his phone from his pocket. He quickly tapped on it and showed her an audio recording. "Remember, I have a habit of recording all my calls."

"What is this about?" she asked. He tapped on the play button in response. The moment she heard the audio, she knew what it was all about. She felt the ground slipping beneath her feet the moment *his* words hit her ears.

'*S-S-Sona…J-J-J-just listen to me once…*' She heard Kartik's recorded voice and instantly felt sick. She noticed the pain in his voice that she had failed to see that day.

'*Don't you dare to come near me. What do you think of yourself? I don't love you, I never loved you and will never love a person like you. It really doesn't matter to me if you jump from here or hang yourself or do whatever with yourself. People like you are nothing but a burden on earth.'* After that, there was a bustle and then complete silence. It had been her voice. Reeva remembered each and every word that she had said to him before he took his life. She didn't say a word more and stood there motionless.

He came forward and clenched her shoulders tightly with his hands. "You destroyed me. You destroyed my whole family. You killed him, Kartik, my little brother," he paused and closed his eyes, as if recreating his brother's image in his mind. "You killed everyone I loved." He gritted his teeth and his brows rutted in anger. "And now, you know the pain when everyone accuses you of something you never did, and no one believes you. Not even your own parents. You too had accused him of something that he never did. You used him and then threw him away like trash. Why did you do that? What was the reason, Kriti?" He cringed as he called her by her real name, as if it tasted bitter on his tongue. "He would have given anything to you without you even asking for it, then why did you do that to him?" He shook his head still looking at her in disgust. "Since the very first day he told me about you, I knew that you were with him only for his money, but he was happy, damn happy, and I would have spent every last penny that I had for that one smile that you put on his face. That is where I went wrong, and you committed the same mistake too. You had sensed in the very beginning that I wasn't good for you, nonetheless you trusted me. I could have stopped him, but I didn't. You could have stopped yourself, but you didn't. I will live out the rest of my life in pain and regret, and now, you too will live with the same remorse. You not only took his life, but my parents' too. Because of you, I have to live out my life without my family and without any purpose in life, and now, you too are all alone. What will you do now, Reeva? Will you jump off of the same building?"

She looked at him with teary eyes. She had never imagined that she would have to confront her past like that someday. She could have screamed, she could have fought with him, she could have yelled at him for doing all this to her, she could have run far enough from him to save herself from further pain, but she didn't. She was too shocked to do any of that. Either that, or perhaps she had already accepted all his accusations. She considered herself responsible for his pain.

For a moment, she felt numb. She couldn't hear what he said next. The only thing she could feel was his vibe laced with loathing and frustration. She stood there motionless, while he kept yelling at her how she had ruined his life. Soon he was gone, having left her all alone with so many blames. She walked over to the spot from where Kartik had jumped off four years back. Had she really been the reason behind his suicide? All this time, she had convinced herself that she wasn't responsible for his death; instead, it was he who had killed the girl she was before. He had given her enough reason to take her own life too, but she had been strong. She wasn't a coward like him. It's okay to give up on a dream, a love, or even a hope, but it's not okay to give up on life because that's irrevocable. She looked down from the building and suddenly, the scene from that day flashed in front of her eyes.

"You were a coward, do you hear me? I didn't kill you, your cowardice did. What did you think? That your decision to end your life would make me fall in love with you? No. I hate you even more now. You ruined my life," she yelled and closed her eyes. The pained face of Agnivesh flashed in front of her eyes. "You ruined many lives," she sobbed. She turned and sat down, resting her back against the barricade. She started to feel sick suddenly and covered her mouth with her hands. A feeling of intense nausea took over her and she rushed downstairs to the washroom, but before she could reach it, she threw up all over the stairs. She sank down to a step, holding the railing, and went limp. She didn't know for how long she sat there, but next, she found herself standing outside her home and ringing the bell continuously. The door opened and she saw her mother standing there, stunned to see Reeva in this state.

"What happened, Reeva?" Sumitra asked, and Reeva whimpered. Sumitra quickly hefted Reeva's wilting body as she staggered into her arms. Sumitra took her inside and made her lie in bed. Reeva instantly curled into a disheveled heap and poured out her pain in the form of uncontrollable cries. She closed her eyes and an image of Kartik, happy and smiling, swarmed in her head.

'*Stay away from him, Kriti. You have no idea how belligerent he is! No one talks to him in this college because he is a psycho. He has no control over his anger. I am telling you, you will regret it one day. He is just using you to show you off as his girlfriend in front of everyone*." The warning from Gayatri and Vikrant echoed in her head. They had repeatedly warned her to stay away from Kartik, but she hadn't listened to them. How could she have ever believed that the guy who was so sweet to her could betray her? She squeezed her eyes shut and sobbed. No matter how hard she tried to efface it, each and every detail of that day remained etched in her heart. She had gone to Gayatri and Vikrant's engagement that day when Gayatri told her that a surprise was waiting for her at the terrace. The scene from that day flashed in front of her eyes, vivid and clear.

*She reached the terrace; the door was open, so she paved her way to find the surprise that Gayatri had mentioned. Not that she was interested in any surprises at that moment, but something in her gut told her to go ahead. She had only taken a few steps when she saw him standing there in one corner, on a call with someone.* Now she understood that he had been on a call with Agnivesh. *Panic gushed all over her face. The last thing she had expected was to find Kartik there. She had been avoiding him since the day he broke her trust. She froze to see him standing in front of her. Her body shuddered. She wanted to run, but couldn't. She felt like her feet were trapped in a quagmire and she was sinking down with every passing second. Kartik sensed her presence behind him and turned to look at her with teary eyes. As he closed the distance between them, she gathered her courage and pushed him hard. He stumbled back by a few steps and she took the chance to run away, but he caught her just in time. His phone slipped out of his hand however.*

*"S-S-Sona...J-J-J-just listen to me once," he said, still holding her hand, while she tried to wriggle out of his grasp. She knew already what he wanted to say. He had been sending her several messages on her phone over the past few days, saying that he loved her and that he would kill himself if she didn't respond. Consequently, she had to block his number. She used all her strength and yanked her hand out of his grip.*

*"Don't you dare come near me. What do you think of yourself? I don't love you, I never loved you and will never love a person like you. It really doesn't matter to me if you jump from here or hang yourself or do whatever with yourself. People like you are nothing but a burden on earth," she said and turned to leave. She had descended just a few steps when she heard a loud bang. She knew instantly that he was gone, but she didn't turn back. She felt too numb to feel any emotion, as if she had turned into a corpse. She felt too smothered to even cry. Her body was shaking with fear and agony. She reached home in the same state and since then, stopped living her life.*

Impetuously, she had lashed out all her rage at him. She had never imagined that he would take such a drastic step. He was gone forever. She had been so absorbed in her own sorrow that it never came to her mind that Kartik had a family too. She now learnt in a bitter way that the day he was gone, she wasn't the only one to have lost him. Agnivesh had lost everything too. She had always sensed Agnivesh to be broken just like her, but she didn't know that they both had been broken for the same reason, for the same person. She didn't have any grudges against Agnivesh. His loss was far greater than hers. Her heart cried for him. She cried for the pain he had endured all this while, until darkness took over her and she fell into a deep slumber.

***

# All About Sona

20 May, 2012

*Dear Diary,*

*I am filling you after more than a month. Remember, the last time I wrote in you, I had a broken hand because of the fight. I didn't realize then that it had caused a boxer's fracture near my knuckle, hence my hand had been bandaged. So much happened in this one month. I came to know so many things about her. I also told her so many things about me. I discussed something with her that I have never talked about with anyone. My biggest grief. I told her how much I loved participating in debates and how much I miss it. I am belligerent not because I am a psycho, but because I always have so much to say and when I can't, I use my anger to express it. She listened to everything patiently, then told me something that made me fall in love with her even more. Her exact words were:*

*'Life is not about what you couldn't do, rather it is about what you can still do; it's not about the broken and unfulfilled dreams, rather it is about seeing a new dream every day. So what if you can't participate in debates anymore, you can still use your knowledge to debate in writing. Why don't you start writing a blog or something, where you can make your point and dump all those thoughts that are the cause of so much fury inside you?'*

*Wasn't it simple? Why did I never think about writing before? Our relationship has bloomed since then, as we have started discussing serious things too. And now, I feel confident enough to propose to her. I have planned everything. My birthday is in two days, and that's when I am going to propose to her. And you know what? She has already bought a gift for me. Last week, when I told her about my birthday, she was so excited that the very next day she asked me about my favorite brand of T-shirt, and we went to VR mall in my Porsche to shop. I love seeing her sitting beside me while I drive. I told her my size and let her choose the design for me. After shortlisting a few T-shirts, she asked me to try them on. She selected three out of them, then asked me to pick one. I chose the yellow one. Do you know why? Because it reminded me of the day I saw her for the first time. She was wearing the same kind of yellow collar neck T-shirt that day. She bought it instantly using my card, while reiterating that she would return the money after getting a job. She doesn't know that I hardly care for money. Moreover, my brother will be paying the bills, and he is earning in abundance these days.*

*I also invited her to my house for my birthday. I want her to see the place where I have grown up. She agreed right away. I didn't tell her that there would be just the two of us. I don't like throwing a big party on my birthday, as I hardly have any friends. Every year on my birthday, my parents organize a charity event. They started it after my accident as a gesture to thank God for saving my life. I used to join them initially, but then I stopped going, and they never forced me. I have been spending my birthday evenings all alone for the last five years. But this time, I am going to spend it with Sona. And I am really looking forward to it.*

# 13

"Good morning, sir," Agnivesh's secretary Menasha stood up as he made his way to his office in Mumbai. He didn't respond and headed straight to his cabin, closing the door behind him. Once inside, he slammed his hand on the table. He was angry, but he didn't know the reason. Was he angry because he wasn't able to break Reeva the way he had wanted to? Or even worse, was he angry with himself for trying to break her in the first place? Every time he saw her looking at him with those gloomy eyes, every fiber of his body cursed him for giving her that pain. He wasn't supposed to fall in love with her; he was supposed to hate her for having ruined his life, his family. Yet, he had fallen in love with her the moment he saw her for the first time.

The way she stood in front of him, confident and poised, had made him question his own motives. The raw beauty that defined her charisma had floored him. No wonder, his brother had been head over heels in love with this girl. The fact that she wasn't even trying to impress him with fancy dress, makeup or conversation had made her even more distinctive. How could someone look so divine on the outside, yet be so cruel from the inside? Even though he tried hard to suppress the emotions that were slowly creeping up his nerves, he couldn't help it. He rounded the large wooden table and sat in his chair. He picked up his phone and informed his secretary not to disturb him until further orders. He leaned forward and rubbed his temples. After meeting Reeva on the terrace of The Grand Rajvilaas, he had come straight to his Mumbai office. He knew that if he had stayed there any longer, he would have melted and tried to check if she was okay.

*I love you.*

Those words had been haunting him since the day Reeva confessed her love for him. Hearing it aloud from her had healed and devastated him at the same time. He felt undeserving of that emotion. He felt unworthy of the role she was ready to give him in her life. The night he had consummated his relationship, fake relationship, with her flashed in front of his eyes. That night, they hadn't just fit perfectly, but she also seemed to have consumed every cell of his body. He had the urge to forgive her and start afresh. It wasn't easy on him, as he knew well what she had done to his brother, yet he considered giving her another chance. People change with time and deserve a second chance in life, don't they? He knew that he was being selfish there, but somehow it felt the right thing to do. That night, if she had told him just once that she regretted what she did to his brother, he would have forgiven her, but she had explicitly stated that she had no regrets. And that was the last straw. In that moment, whatever feelings he had developed for her vanished, and the only thing that remained was hatred. Pure hatred. All he wanted thereafter was to give her the same pain that he had been going through.

He opened his drawer and took out an old photograph of him with his family. It was perhaps the last time they had all been together, almost ten years ago. He still remembered the day he left his home. His father's words still reverberated in his ears. '*All my life, I nurtured this business in the hope that one day you will take it to new heights, but you have grown so mature now that you are ashamed to have your name linked to it. And now, I am ashamed to have my name linked with you. This business is me, and if you are going to leave it, you will also have to leave me, my name and all other people related to me. Go and live your dream, and forget that you ever had a family.*'

Agnivesh had known that once he left his house, all doors would be closed for him forever. Though Solanki was their surname, Agnivesh and Kartik never used it. Instead, they used Adiraaj, their father's name, as their surname. He knew well what his father had meant when he asked him to leave his name. That day, Agnivesh Adiraaj became Agnivesh Solanki. The pain that he had seen in his father's eyes that day still pricked at his heart. He had left his home and his family behind with a promise that he would make them proud one day, and that they would themselves call him back. He wanted to prove to his father that he wasn't ashamed to have his name linked to his business. Instead, he just wanted to make his father proud of having his name linked to Agnivesh's business. He worked hard to get there as soon as possible, so that he might return to his family soon. Alas! That day never came. He missed all of them with every breath he took.

The same year, his younger brother Kartik met with an accident. He came back to them then, but his father didn't allow him to enter. Due to the huge age difference between him and his brother, he had shared almost a fatherly bond with Kartik. He craved to see his little brother once, but his father didn't let him.

Sitting in his leather chair, he winced at the memory of that day. Then, a soft smile crept onto his face as he remembered the day his brother called him for the first time after two years. Agnivesh had been in profound shock upon learning about the impaired speech of his brother. He knew what an enthusiast he was about debating championships, and God had indeed been cruel to him by snatching away the only thing he loved.

Somewhere, Agnivesh held himself responsible for his loss. Perhaps, if he had been with him that day, it wouldn't have happened to his little brother. Kartik kept calling him occasionally, without the knowledge of their father. He was growing, so were his needs. Their father had always been strict and vigilant about where his kids were spending money, so Agnivesh gifted Kartik his own credit card on his eighteenth birthday. He remembered how happy his brother had been that day. However, he kept a close eye on how he was spending the money. One day, he called his brother when he noticed that he had shopped for some women's clothing online using his card. It irked him, as Kartik had never done anything like that before. That was the day he first learnt about the girl in his life. With the way she was shopping through his credit card, it didn't take him much time to realize that the girl was with Kartik only for the money. He wanted to warn Kartik, but he was so smitten. The conversation that he had had with him then was still clear in his head.

*"Why are you shopping for female clothing?" I asked.*

*"I-I-It's not me, S-Sona b-bought some d-d-dresses for herself," he said.*

*"Who is Sona?"*

*"F-F-Friend,"*

*"Friend or girlfriend?" I teased him.*

*"F-Friend," he paused and then added, "b-b-but I l-like her."*

*"Look Kartik, I am not acting dad here, but I want to tell you something. It's normal to have infatuations at the age you are in, but don't get too involved," I said.*

*"D-d-don't worry, b-bhai. She is a nice g-g-girl."*

*"I am sure, take care," I said before disconnecting the phone.*

His brother was finally happy after a long time and no amount of money matched up to his brother's happiness for him. Everything was going fine, until the day a few months later when he received a call from Kartik. The hair on the nape of his neck stood up as he ruminated over that conversation.

*"Sh-Sh-She left me..." Kartik trailed off and sobbed. My heartbeat spiked up immediately as I heard him crying. Had I not been on the other side of the globe, I would have rushed to him right away. I closed my eyes, sinking in helplessness. Hadn't I always known that this day was approaching? Yet, I had let him drown in that emotion.*

*"It's okay, Kartik. It's her loss. I knew that she would do this to you, that's why I told you not to get too involved," I tried to calm him down.*

*"Sh-Sh-She will never c-c-come back. She said that I-I tried to a-a-abuse her physically," he said, and I sprang up from my seat in reflex.*

*"Did you?" I asked, clenching my hand in a fist.*

*"N-N-No. Do you think I can do a-a-anything like that with h-her, or any other g-g-girl for that matter?" he replied. Pain was palpable in his voice, and I hated that girl even more in that moment. She was lying through her teeth, without thinking twice what harm her single lie was causing my brother.*

*"Even D-D-Dad thinks I d-d-did that to her. N-N-now, how am I s-s-suppose to l-l-live with that?" he added. Oh! So she had even taken Dad into her confidence. I could imagine what Kartik must have been going through, now that Dad believed her too.*

*"Don't worry. I trust you, and I am with you. You just calm down," I tried to appease him.*

*"I-I-I was just a-a-angry at h-her. I l-loved her w-with everything I had, and she left me f-for s-s-someone else," he sobbed again.*

*"Don't worry, brother. I will make everything all right. I promise you that," I said, placing my hand over my heart.*

*"R-Really? But h-how?" he sounded hopeful all of a sudden.*

*"I am coming back home," I said the words that had been lingering on my tongue for quite some time. "I have realized, Kartik, nothing is more important than family. Even success feels hollow when you have no one to celebrate with. I wasn't competing with Dad; rather, I just wanted to make him proud of me. So finally, I am coming back home, even if I have to sacrifice my dreams for it," I added, and heard his smile from the other end.*

*"M-Mom will be so h-h-happy. Not a s-single day goes by when she doesn't t-t-talk about you," he said.*

*"I know."*

*"And y-y-you will bring b-b-back Sona too?" he asked again.*

*"I can't promise you that, but I promise that I will make everything all right," I said. I promised myself that I would never let that girl come back into my brother's life, but I would surely help him move on.*

*"I know, n-n-no one can d-do anything. She w-won't c-come back," he sniveled again.*

No matter how hard Agnivesh tried to calm him down, nothing could placate him.

Since that day, he started calling Kartik daily. Agnivesh was happy that his brother was finally moving on, until the day he again received a call from his brother at an odd hour. As he picked up the call, he conjectured from the bustle at the other end that the call had been connected by mistake. He was about to hang up when he heard his brother. Pain was so palpable in Kartik's voice that Agnivesh instantly stood up from his seat, as if he knew that something ominous was about to happen. Then he heard her voice, the girl he used to call Sona. There was so much hatred in her voice that he clenched his fists upon hearing it, and so tightly that his knuckles turned white. His biggest fear had come true that day. Before he could do anything, sitting half a world away, Kartik had jumped from the terrace of that high-rise building. He died instantly. There was a suicide note in his pocket that clearly declared that he was ending his life because he was tired of it and that he didn't hold anyone responsible for it.

Agnivesh left for Surat immediately. When he landed at the airport, he received a call from his father's PA, Manish, who informed him that his brother had committed suicide, and that his father had suffered a cardiac arrest and had been admitted to a hospital. His whole world came crashing down around him in that one moment. By the time he reached the hospital, his father had already left the world. He felt even more devastated when he saw his mother sitting motionless in a chair in one corner of the hospital room. When he went to sit beside her, she didn't even look up at him once. The moment he held her hand, he realized that something was wrong. Her fingernails had turned blue, her breathing was shallow, and she was not responding to his touch anymore. The traumatic experience that she had just endured had affected her in a sever manner.

Though the doctors tried their level best to save her, she died after a month long struggle in the coma. His whole world had come to an end, and all because of that one girl. He knew nothing about her then. His brother had never told him anything about her, except her name—*Sona*, which turned out to be a fake name. He had never tried to prod further. He hadn't imagined even in his worst dream that everything would spiral out of his control this way.

He didn't even know her real name. With no name or identity, it became almost impossible for him to find that girl. There were times when he even doubted her existence. It took him several years to reach her. He dug out her name and address via the online purchases she had made, though it wasn't easy because of the strict privacy policies of the shopping sites. He got to know that the girl's name was Kriti Panchal, but when he reached at her address, he found out through the neighbors that the girl along with her family had left that place a few months back, and no one knew where they had gone. He hadn't thought that it would be so difficult to find her, but the girl had changed her name as well as address. Why would anyone do that if they weren't guilty? He kept in touch with her old neighbors and offered them a hefty amount in exchange for any information about her. One day, after almost three years, one of them called Agnivesh and told him about her whereabouts. They had recognized her from her profile on a matrimonial site. He put everything he had earned on stake, just to find her out.

When he approached her, it was with the assumption that money would be enough to lure her into his plan. But he was wrong. Rather, everything he had assumed about her turned out to be false. His money or reputation didn't affect any of her decisions. Rather, she didn't give a damn about his affluence. Agnivesh started doubting if she was even the same girl who had been with his brother. But the night she spent with him at his hotel room for the first time, she murmured his brother's name in her sleep and he knew right away that she was the one.

She had fooled the world, but she couldn't fool her own conscience that kept reminding her of her sins. Despite trying hard to go the opposite way, Agnivesh had started to develop a soft corner for her, which is why he pushed her away every time she tried to come close to him. He maintained his distance so that he wouldn't develop feelings for her. The night he executed the final stage of his plan, he found himself weak in his resolve. He even distanced himself from her, cursing himself for doing wrong to her.

When he went back to meet her at the hotel where Reeva confessed her feelings for him, he strayed from his intentions. Consummating their relationship was his biggest mistake. For a while, he even decided to forgive her and start afresh with her, but the moment she confessed that she didn't regret anything in life, including what she had done to his brother, he was back to being himself. He went back to his original plan. He left the hotel room knowing full well what was to come next. He had purposely chosen that hotel. Being in the same business, he knew which hotel was running what kind of a business.

More than a month had passed since that day, yet somewhere deep in his gut, he felt that he had wronged that girl. Every time his mind attempted to convince him that she deserved all of it, his heart came up with its own reasons.

He placed his hands behind his head and leaned back in his chair. He didn't realize when a tear dropped down to stain his cheek. His phone rang and he picked it up immediately, seeing Manish's number on it. Agnivesh had instructed him to keep a close eye on Reeva, dreading that she might do something wrong. She was the strongest girl he had ever known. When he had seen her at the expo the previous day, smiling and dealing with the crowd exuberantly, a part of him had surged with fury, while the other part had swelled with pride upon seeing her willpower.

Manish's voice from the other end broke his reverie. "Mr. Solanki, we have got hold of the property where Ms. Reeva Panchal is running her workshop."

“Good, anything else?”

“Nothing for now.”

“Did she turn up in her workshop today?”

“No. She didn’t.”

“Make sure we have our own lock on that property before she shows up there tomorrow.”

“Certainly.”

He disconnected the call and resumed his work.

***

# 14

The next day, when Reeva was getting ready for work, she felt queasy again. She rushed to the washroom and tried to throw up, but nothing dribbled out. She hadn't eaten anything the previous day, despite her mother's repeated pleas. Though she felt unwell, what surprised her was that even after going through so much the day before, she had woken up without any nightmares about that fateful day. She picked up her bag and headed towards the main door of the house.

She had just reached the living room when she heard her father say, "Sumitra, tell her that there is no need to go back to that place again. If she wants to live here, she has to leave the work she is doing."

She understood what her father was referring to. How could she have forgotten that they still didn't trust her?!

"I am sorry for showing up unannounced yesterday. I assure you, it won't happen again," Reeva said, while her throat got choked with the emotions she was trying to hold. Prakash looked at her fiercely, while Sumitra attempted to calm the matter down.

"Reeva, you are our only child. We would never want to hurt you or do anything that is not good for you. Please try to understand."

"Do you trust me?" asked Reeva.

"Yes, we do. But we have to live in this society, and we can't be ignorant towards it. You have no idea how we've spent this past month without you. There wasn't a single day when we didn't cry for you. We aren't the villain here," Sumitra said, sobbing. Reeva knew well that they weren't the villains of her story. Rather, no one was, except the situations.

Reeva held her mother's hand instantly and said, "But telling me that I can't do what I love doing the most proves it otherwise, Maa. I feel happy when I am at that place. Don't make me choose. Please."

"Happy? Bullshit! You think it makes you happy? You wouldn't have come here in the state you were in yesterday if it gave you any happiness. To make matter worse, you named your business from the letter *K*," Sumitra seethed. Reeva wanted to argue, but kept her mouth shut. She had wanted to argue that day too when her mother forced her to change her name from Kriti to Reeva, just because an astrologer suggested that 'K' wasn't going well with her stars. She never told them exactly what had happened that day. She never told them why she left her studies. She never explained to them why she had spent six whole months holed up in her room. She had been so depressed that she didn't want to meet anyone. Painting was the only thing that gave her a little respite from all the despair.

Her father's friend helped her to get a job at a call center, which bolstered her confidence to mingle with the outside world again. She had made so many paintings over this time that keeping them all in her small house became difficult. She started *Kreative Krafts* with the intention to get rid of all those paintings, and also help her father financially. She had purposely chosen a name with the letter 'K' for her business to prove to her parents that a letter had nothing to do with one's destiny. She didn't realize how she got so attached to her business over time that giving up on it was akin to giving up on life itself.

Her phone buzzed in her handbag, She pulled it out and saw Raghu's name flashing on the screen. She was late already, so she picked up the phone instantly.

"Raghu, I am on my way. You have the keys, right?" she said over the phone.

"Yes, I do. But this lock isn't ours, and all our things are lying outside the workshop," he replied.

"What do you mean by *outside the workshop*?" Reeva's heart started throbbing in her chest.

"I don't know, Didi. Have you paid the rent?" he asked.

"Of course, I have. Let me talk to the landlord," she said and disconnected the call. She called up her landlord, Mr. Goradia, right away. He picked the call on the first ring itself.

"Jai Shri Krishna, Reeva. I know why you have called me, and I am really sorry for everything. You know how deserted that place is, and I got such an amazing offer for it that I couldn't resist. I have sold that place. You won't believe it, the person paid triple the value of that house."

"How can you do that? We had an agreement, and you can't turn it down without prior notice."

"I know that, but the person who bought it needed possession immediately, so I had to do it. Don't worry, you will get your compensation."

"It's not about the compensation; it's about my business. What will I do now? Where will I go?" Reeva yelled at him.

“I really can’t do anything. Why don’t you talk to the person who has bought the house, maybe he will agree to let you work there for some time till you find a better arrangement.”

“Can you send me his number?” said Reeva, pressing the bridge of her nose.

“Yes, sure.”

Reeva disconnected the phone, and her screen flashed with a message from her landlord a minute later. She quickly tapped on the number, then clicked on the call option. Her jaw ticked and eyes glazed over as she saw Agnivesh’s name flashing on the screen. Why was she so surprised to know that he had done this to her? She looked at her parents who were already looking at her with so many questions in their eyes.

“Hello, Reeva. Oh! Sorry, Kriti. I was actually waiting for your call,” Reeva heard Agnivesh’s voice from the other end. She quickly pivoted and rushed into her room. Bolting it from the inside, she replied, “Why? You know what that place means to me,” she said. No matter how hard she tried to sound confident, her voice jittered nonetheless. She heard him laughing humorlessly on the other side.

“Of course, I know. That’s why I did it. You know, we never understand the pain of others until we experience it ourselves. I want you to experience how this pain feels. It had taken my father twenty seven years to raise his business, and then everything was gone in the blink of an eye. I am sure you can feel now what I had felt at that time,” he said.

“I am not the reason behind any of your sufferings.” Reeva gathered all her courage and poured out everything she had hidden in her heart. “Did you hear that? I am not the reason. Rather, it was your brother who broke me into pieces, who broke my trust. Do you want to know what he did with me? He tried to rape me”—she closed her eyes as a tear rolled down her cheek—"and he would have succeeded had your father not come in on time. And you know what, instead of scolding him, your father blamed me and called me a whore." She slowly slid down against the wall as she cried her heart out.

"What rubbish?! I don't believe you. It was you who put false allegations on him and abetted him to take his life. He would never have done that, I know him well," he growled.

"That's what I had thought too, that I knew him well, when I agreed to go to his house for his birthday celebration. But guess what, he had planned that purposely to trap me there," she sobbed.

"For God's sake, Reeva, stop making up stories. He is dead now," he said, and she could hear him pacing.

"Yes. I know. I can't prove anything now, no one can, but I just want you to know that I wasn't the reason. Just because he died and I didn't, doesn't mean he was right and I am wrong." And with that, she ended the call. Surprisingly, she felt far lighter after having let her heart out, even though Agnivesh didn't believe her.

***

# 15

Agnivesh paced apprehensively in his room in Mumbai. He was completely shaken by Reeva's confession. It wasn't something he didn't know before, but hearing it from her own mouth had knocked him off-kilter. He knew that it could never be true. He knew his brother well, and more than that, he believed in his upbringing. She had blamed not only his brother, but also his father, whereas he clearly remembered Kartik mentioning that their father believed her and not him. '*I shouldn't believe her, that girl is lying*,' he whispered to himself, yet he couldn't ignore the quiver in her voice when she had confessed. What if all that turned out to be true? Would he ever be able to forgive himself for what he had done with the girl who had already been wronged by his own family? He rubbed his chest as the pain started to pierce his heart. He had experienced a lot in his life to read a lie in one's voice. And in Reeva's case, his heart refused to admit that she was lying.

*I can't prove anything now, no one can, but I just wanted you to know that I wasn't the reason. Just because he died and I didn't, doesn't mean he was right and I am wrong.*

Her words ricocheted in his ears and weighed heavy on his heart. He felt as if there was no way for him to ever be able to find the truth. He sat on the couch and closed his eyes. He played everything that had happened till then in his mind to find a clue. Nothing. He couldn't come up with any conclusion. Then suddenly, he ruminated over Reeva's father's version of the story: *She didn't take her grandfather's death well. I still remember that fateful day. It was the same day she met with an accident while coming home by auto. She had a wound on the side of her forehead and bruises all over her body.*

Hadn't it happened on 22 May? Kartik's birthday. And it was the same day when something major changed in Reeva's life. He quickly called his driver and told him to get ready to leave for Surat. He needed to talk to Reeva if he wanted to dig the truth out. Hours flew by, and he found himself standing outside his house where he had spent his whole childhood. It was past eight in the night, so he decided to meet Reeva the next day.

He instantly felt goosebumps as he opened the door and entered his home. He had promised his father that he would never enter this house again, and he hadn't, except the one time to perform the last rites of his father and his brother. He had hired people to make sure that the house was regularly cleaned and maintained. Memories flashed in front of his eyes as if it all had happened just yesterday. Though he was proud of his achievements, regardless he felt that the cost he had to pay for his success was far more than what he got in return. The time spent with his own family would have been his real achievement, but he had run after those materialistic possessions that his success brought him. He had always thought that once he was successful, he would have enough time to convince and make up with his family. But he had been so wrong. He touched the dining table where they used to have their meals together. It used to be him and his brother, as they were always served their meals before their parents. The living room, the TV room, the kitchen, everything took him back to the times he had been ruminating in his mind since he left the place. He couldn't gather enough courage to enter his parents' or his brother's room, and strolled towards his room. It had been almost ten years since he last entered his room.

He was surprised to see that it was kept exactly the way he had left it. His furniture, his wardrobe, his posters, everything was untouched. He smiled wistfully as he reminisced what his brother had told him once, that their mother used to sleep in his room whenever their father wasn't home. This had been her way to feel his presence near her. He walked over to his wardrobe and brushed his hand over a poster that was still sticking there. It was a handwritten warning for his little brother to not touch his almirah. He had taken that warning so seriously that he never even let their mother touch the almirah.

He opened it and found some clothes hanging there; some of them were his, while some he recognized as his brothers. He could see that there were plenty of things that perhaps belonged to his brother. Kartik had told him that their mother had started spying through his room, so he had started keeping some things in this almirah so that their mother wouldn't find out. His gaze then landed on a diary hidden behind all the clothes. It caught his attention because of the name embossed on it. It was from the Agni group of hotels that Agnivesh had sent to his brother almost five years ago. He was sure that it would be the only thing in this house that bore the name of his hotel group. He opened it and found just three words scribbled on the first page: *All About Sona.*

***

# All About Sona

23 May, 2012

*Dear Diary,*

*Today as I am writing this, I am crying. Can you imagine? I AM CRYING! Me! I never thought I had any feelings in my system other than anger. But after meeting Sona, I realized I could feel love too. And now, she has evoked this new emotion in me. She left me wrecked. Heartbroken. Devastated. Everything is finished. She is gone. I have ruined everything. I had been so excited for yesterday, my birthday, but nothing of that sort happened.*

*Remember, I had invited Sona home. She told me that she would come a little late in the evening, as she had some urgent work before. I trusted her, but she betrayed me. She didn't have any urgent work; instead, she had gone to meet someone else. She was on a date with someone else, and I would never have believed it had I not seen her with him myself. I was waiting for her. I had even decorated my room with candles and flowers, as I had planned to propose to her there. When she didn't arrive even after eight in the evening, I called her, and she said she was on her way. I was eagerly waiting for her. Standing on my balcony, my eyes remained glued to the road. Then, I saw a bike stopping in front of my gate. I recognized her sitting behind. She got down and rounded the bike to stand in front of the person who was riding it. I couldn't recognize him as he was wearing a helmet. He removed his helmet and I was stunned to see who it was. Raunak.*

*But what surprised me more was that he was wearing the same yellow T-shirt that she had bought for me... or perhaps I had misunderstood the whole thing, maybe she never bought it for me. My heart sank. But it was nothing compared to what I saw next, it left my blood boiling. I saw them kissing goodbye. The vein in my head started throbbing, looking at this sight. I felt rage scorching my body. I fisted my hands in an attempt to control my anger, but I was losing all control over myself. I tried to calm myself down, thinking that I might have mistaken the gesture, that there was nothing between them, but the thing is...I know Sona, and I know that she would never let anyone touch her, unless...*

*The doorbell rang and I dashed to open the door. As I opened it, her smiling face calmed me down a bit. She warbled the birthday wishes and hugged me. But I was so hot eared by then that even her saccharine voice stung me. She rummaged through her handbag and took out a box. Opening it, she showed me a wristwatch, then proceeded to tie it on my hand. She sensed that something was wrong with me. "What happened to you?" she asked, but I had nothing to tell her. I knew that I wouldn't be able to discuss anything without lashing out anger. I decided to keep quiet and invited her inside. She was surprised to see that I hadn't invited anyone else.*

*I told her to come to my room, and she agreed. Listening to her talk, I decided to forget everything for the day and revel in the moment. After all, she was here at my house. I poured some wine into two glasses, as she had once told me that she wanted to try it. She took a sip and grimaced, "It tastes horrible," but then she pressed her nose with her fingers and gulped down the whole glass at once. She looked at me then and said, "You know, I am so happy today." She stretched the 'so' and my mind displayed again the image of her kissing that boy on the street.*

*"Who did you come here with?" I asked, even though I had already recognized him.*

*"You saw him? It was Raunak. Remember? He studies in your college only," she said, and I just nodded nonchalantly. Talking about him so enthusiastically, did she even realize*

*that she was hurting me? "If you had asked me about him yesterday, I would have introduced him as my crush, but today, I can introduce him as my boyfriend. And you know what? You are the first one to know about this," she continued, blushing. I had to literally bite my tongue to maintain my composure.*

*My mouth felt dry, so I picked up my glass of wine and drained the whole fill in one big gulp. My throat burned, but it was nothing compared to my burning heart. My jaw clenched. My muscles tensed. And for one moment, I felt as if I would break the glass in my hand. "You know, it's my first relationship, and on the first day, the very first date, I got a kiss too," she said. A sudden fury coursed through my veins and I couldn't handle it anymore. I didn't even realize how or when my hand flew towards her and I slapped her hard across her face.*

*My first mistake.*

*Losing her balance, she stumbled to one side and hit her head on the side of the table before falling to the ground. Flabbergasted, she looked at me as she raised herself up on her palms. "Are you mad? How dare you hit me?" she grumbled and sprang up on her feet. "You psycho," she yelled, dashing towards me. She pushed me, and I slapped her one more time.*

*My second mistake.*

*This time, she tumbled to the side of my bed. I grabbed her by the elbow and pulled her up. Before she could yank it away, I wrapped my arms around her tightly and tried to kiss her.*

*My third mistake.*

*She wriggled in my arms as she tried to push me away, but I was too strong against her. I looked into her eyes and saw tears streaming down. I could see panic spreading all over her face. Then I saw the trickle of blood running down the side of her head. What had I done to this girl? I had hit her. She was bleeding from her forehead. The realization hit me hard. Releasing her, I took a step back. I had promised myself that I would never hurt this girl, yet I had hit her. She also took a step back and tried to run out, but I pounced at her and grabbed her by her waist. I couldn't let her go with that impression of me in her mind. I knew that if she left at that moment, she would never come back.*

*So, I did what I felt most appropriate at that time, and it was indeed a Himalayan blunder. I tried to stop her and tell her that I loved her. She squealed and tried to break free from my hold. Then suddenly, she stomped down hard on my foot. My grip around her loosened and she stumbled forward on the floor. To prevent her from escaping, I lunged forward and pushed my weight onto her. She tried to wrestle as I shifted my body over her and trapped her by gripping her arms above her head with my hand and pinning her thighs with my knees.*

*I tried to tell her that I didn't want to hurt her, that I loved her, and that I just wanted to talk to her, but the uprising anxiety had choked my already impaired speech. Without trying to understand me, she started screaming for help. I wanted her to listen to me, so I covered her mouth with my hand to muffle her screams, not realizing that I was smothering her. Just then, the door of my room flung open and I saw my father standing there with his jaw dropped.*

*I instantly released her and stood up on my feet. She curled up in a foetal position and started sobbing, burying her head in her arms. Her gut-wrenching sobs felt like a twisting dagger in my chest. I cursed myself for having given her this pain. My father looked at me angrily as a vein in his forehead throbbed. Then he looked at Sona and grumbled, "Get up. Fast."*

*She rose and sat up on the ground, still crying. "What the hell is going on here?" my father asked, glaring at Sona. She looked up at him as fresh tears pooled in her eyes. Hiding her face in her palms, she sobbed. "He was trying to harass me," she blubbered. I looked at her stunned. I wasn't trying to harass her, I had just wanted to talk to her. But what my father said next was definitely some harassment.*

*"He was harassing you? Did he kidnap you? Did he force you to come to his house and his room at this hour?" he asked, and she shook her head. "Did he force you to drink?" he asked, looking at the empty wine glasses on the table. She shook her head again in response. "Do you study with him?" he shot another question, and she shook her head yet again. "How long have you known him?" he asked.*

*"Two months," she replied.*

*"And in just two months you've become so comfortable with him that you came to his room all alone at this hour? Do you know what our society calls a girl like you? Now get out and stop playing this victim card. I know your kind of girls very well."*

*I hated my father for all that he said to her. It was my mistake entirely. Her only mistake was that she trusted the wrong person. I opened my mouth to tell him the truth, but he held his hand up to quieten me. "Don't you feel ashamed when you look at yourself in the mirror? Girls like you should die in the wombs of their mothers," he grumbled at her again and I closed my eyes, clenching my hands into fists. Sona stood up and ran out of my room. I started to run behind her, but my father's stern voice stopped me. He pinned me there with his gaze. I couldn't move, but the thought that if she left this place with the impression that I was harassing her, she would never return, gave me power and I ran after her, snubbing my father's commands. By the time I reached the road, she had already hailed an Auto and was away.*

*I stomped back, ready to confront my father, but as soon as I stood in front of him, he slapped me hard. Once. Twice. Thrice. I didn't feel offended. I deserved it. "The girl wasn't lying, do you even realize what you have done? What if she presses charges against you? Your whole life will be spoiled. I have to sort out this matter," he yelled and pivoted to his room. I knew that he would make sure that this incident didn't affect his reputation. I called on Sona's number incessantly, but she didn't pick up. I wanted to discuss this with someone, so I called up my brother and told him everything. I didn't tell him that I had hit her though. He is the only person who loves me and believes in me. I can't afford to lose his trust at this moment. I don't know if I will ever see her again, but I won't give up on her.*

~

# 16

Agnivesh leaned his head back, holding the diary close to his heart. He was sitting in a recliner in his room. It was past midnight, and he had read through the whole diary without blinking. His eyes seared from the continuous reading and chest ached with regret. Coldness started seeping into his heart and numbness dragged him into an inferno. He realized that Reeva hadn't been lying, neither was he when he said his brother couldn't ever do that. Sometimes, situations are the devil in our story, and we play the game as per the circumstance. In their case, it had indeed been the situation. The situation had made Kartik a devil in Reeva's story, at the same time making Reeva the devil in Agnivesh's story. They were being played like dummies on strings by the hands of the situation.

He decided to come clean with Reeva first thing in the morning, and let her decide if she wanted to punish him for his behavior or forgive him. He fell asleep on the chair. A few hours later, he felt his phone buzzing somewhere in the room, and he stood up to look for it. He found it on the table near the wardrobe. It was Manish's call. He looked at the time, it was around five in the morning. He was surprised to see him calling at that hour. He picked up the phone.

"What happened?"

"Sir, something went wrong at Reeva's place last evening. There was an ambulance and they have taken someone to the hospital. I have asked someone to collect all the details and will let you know as soon as I get them," he replied, and Agnivesh went numb. What if it was too late to reverse the damage? He had no answer to it, but he wasn't giving up yet. He already regretted what he had made Reeva go through, and he could not let himself be the reason for another disaster in her life.

"Last evening? And you are telling me now?"

"Sir, I came to know about it a bit late, so didn't want to disturb you," he said, and Agnivesh sighed in exasperation.

"Message me the name of the hospital and all the other details that you have," he said and disconnected the call. Rushing out of the house, he called his driver immediately. On the way to the hospital, he received another call from Manish.

"Sir, Reeva was admitted to the hospital. She suddenly fell unconscious."

A wave of apprehension washed over his face as he heard the words. What if she too had done something like his brother? He told the driver to drive faster. His feet continuously tapped the floor of the car in nervousness. He immediately called on Reeva's number, but no one picked up. He even tried her parents' number, but still got the same result.

After about twenty minutes, he reached the hospital. He rushed towards the emergency ward and asked for the room number by giving the receptionist Reeva's credentials. The receptionist gave him her room number, but asked him to fill the visitors' register first. Not paying any attention to that, he sprinted towards her room. As he entered Reeva's room, he found her sitting on the hospital bed. She was dressed in a blue hospital gown and her wrist was pinned with the IV drip. A nurse stood beside her and was checking her blood pressure. Their gazes flew toward him as he knocked on the door.

"What happened to her?" he asked the nurse, but his eyes remained glued to Reeva.

"She suffered from dehydration. Perhaps she wasn't eating and drinking properly," the nurse replied, taking the inflatable cuff of the blood pressure monitor off Reeva's arm. Agnivesh relaxed and heaved a sigh of relief.

"Your blood pressure is still on the higher side. Now lie down and take rest," the nurse instructed Reeva and went out of the room, leaving both of them alone. An awkward silence filled the room. Reeva was aware of his gaze on her, but she refused to look at him, while Agnivesh kept studying her face. She wanted to yell at him and tell him to go away, but she couldn't. He walked over to her and pulled a chair to sit beside her bed. She looked pale and feeble. Her eyes had deep dark circles around them, but the spark in them was still intact. With a little hesitation, he took her hand in his. Reeva didn't look at him, but she neither pull her hand out of his grip.

"I am sorry," he whispered and noticed a frown on her face. She didn't say anything, but slowly closed her eyes.

"Look at me, Reeva. I deserve your anger, take it out on me. Come on, fight me, yell at me, slap me. I know I was wrong, and I am really sorry for it," he said and looked at her expectantly. "Say something, Reeva," he urged.

"I am not angry with you. You were just doing what you felt was right," she finally spoke.

"I should have given you a chance to tell your side of the story."

"You wouldn't have believed me," said Reeva, and he realized that she was perhaps right. He wouldn't have believed her then. But now, he knew that she wasn't wrong.

"Perhaps, but I believe you now," he said.

She looked at him and searched his eyes. "Why this change of heart all of a sudden?" she asked, and Agnivesh silently kept the diary that he had been holding in his hand all this while in her lap.

"What's this?" she asked.

"Open it," he gestured with a nod. As Reeva opened it, her hand flew to her mouth and she gaped at the words. She brushed her fingers over the scribbled letters, *'All about Sona'*.

"I want you to read it. And if possible, forgive him too. He wasn't a bad guy, he just loved you too much," he said. She held the diary tightly in her hands.

"It was my fault too. No matter how much I deny it, but my conscience knows that it was my fault too. I let him fall in love with me when I had never considered him more than a friend," her voice cracked, and she sobbed out the pent-up emotions.

"I assumed that just reminding him repeatedly that we weren't more than friends would be enough. I was just eighteen then. Everything was so new. I wasn't from an affluent family as the other girls in my college. I too wanted the classy clothes and accessories like them. He was fulfilling all my wants, and I was just spending time with him in return. Though I made it clear in every meeting that he was no more than just a friend for me, it wasn't making any difference. I know it was my fault too, and trust me, I curse myself for it every day I wake up. I gave up on my studies and isolated myself from everyone after that," she said and wiped her cheek with the back of her hand, but the tears kept flowing from her eyes. Agnivesh stood up and cupped her face in his palms. He tilted her face up to make her look at him.

"We were all like that at that age, Reeva. Don't curse yourself for anything. It happened because it was destined to happen, and you became the reason. Perhaps we were destined to meet too, because the way we understand each other's pain, no one else ever can. I love you, Reeva. Come back to my life." He smiled and then added, "We are the ones to heal each other, let's be together. Let's face all of it together—" He stopped as he saw Reeva shaking her head.

"No...no...no, you are just confused right now. You are mistaking other emotions for love. It's just regret...or maybe sympathy. But trust me, it' not love," she said, and she looked sure of what she was saying. Agnivesh instantly felt a painful twinge in his gut. How could she say that when she knew nothing about his feelings?

"Give me a chance to bare my heart to you," he said.

"It's not possible, Agnivesh," she replied.

"But that day, you said you loved me. Didn't you?" he asked, searching her eyes, but only to disappoint himself. She looked determined.

"Yes. I had. I had said that to the guy who was there with me that day, and you aren't him. I fell in love with the guy you were pretending to be. But the guy in front of me today is entirely a stranger. I don't know anything about you except your name," she said.

"Okay, then let's give it some time. Take your time to know me and then answer," he said.

"And the answer will still remain the same."

"Why?"

"Because I will never be able to forget what you did to me, how you made me feel that day. No matter how hard I try, I don't think I will ever be able to efface those memories," she said, taking out all the rage that was bugging her inside.

"You know, Reeva, I was angry at that time. I had asked you, and you admitted yourself that you didn't regret anything. I just wanted to fight with you then."

"Then you would have fought me face to face like a man, and not like a coward who left me all alone in that hotel room. Naked. That too on the day I gave you my all. You knew well enough what was coming next, didn't you?" She glared at him, her eyes red and her nose flared. "I will never be able to forgive you for that," she said, shaking her head. She hadn't realized herself how deeply his actions had hurt her.

"Is there anything I can do to undo that? I swear, I will spend the rest of my life making it up to you," he asked.

"A few things can never be undone, no matter how hard you try." She pursed her lips in an attempt to stop her tears and then added, "Like I can't take back all that I said to Kartik that day. I didn't think he would take his life." She held her head between her arms and sobbed hard this time. A sudden knock at the door made Agnivesh turn, while Reeva remained oblivious to it. The nurse rushed to her side and lifted up a glass of water from the side table to her.

"Take small sips, Reeva," she said, offering her the glass. Reeva shoved it away, and a little water splashed on the floor.

"Reeva, look at me. Look, you have to take care of yourself. The way you are handling yourself, it's not good for the baby," the nurse scolded Reeva who was still sobbing silently. *Baby,* the word hung in the air and Agnivesh couldn't stop himself from repeating it.

"Baby," he said, and this time, he got the attention of Reeva too. He looked at her for a moment, then his gaze darted towards the nurse.

"Is she pregnant?" he asked directly, and the nurse replied with a nod. "Almost five weeks," the nurse said. He snapped his gaze back at Reeva and searched her eyes for an answer to the questions that had started to cloud his mind. He conjectured that perhaps Reeva wasn't comfortable talking to him in front of the nurse, so he looked up at her and said, "I will take care of her, can we talk privately for some time?" She nodded and strolled out of the room. As soon as the nurse was gone, he looked at Reeva. "It's my baby. Tell me it's mine," he said, while his heart started thumping loudly in his chest.

"It's mine," she replied, embracing herself in a possessive gesture. She then locked her gaze with him and said, "You know what? Everyone wants me to abort this baby. Do you know why? Because they think that I wouldn't know who the father of this child is. They don't say it, but I can read it in their faces." Tears started pooling in her eyes again. "This is all because of what you did to me that day. And it's not only me who will have to bear the consequences, but this baby too. They think that this baby is nothing but bleak, but I told all of them clearly that I am not going to kill this baby, because it's mine. And see, all of them have left me alone here," she said, staring at the wall blankly.

"I am with you," Agnivesh said, squeezing her hand slightly, but soon realized that she wasn't listening. How could she listen to him when she had so much to say!

"Remember the time you said that you lost your purpose in life and your family because of me? Somewhere, I do hold myself responsible for your loss. Though I never did it intentionally, it still stings my heart. I can't live with it. So I have decided that I will give birth to this baby to return to you your life's purpose. I will bring this baby into this world to give you a family. Perhaps, it will heal the pain of remorse that I feel for you. I will give this baby to you the day he…" she paused and then smiled before adding, "or she is born." She looked at him and found him staring at the ground, still holding her hand in his, lost in his own thoughts. In that moment, she realized that she didn't know whether he even wanted the baby or not.

"Of course, if you want it," she added. He looked up at her and brought her hand to his lips.

"But I need you too," he said before kissing her hand and looking at her hopefully. She pulled her hand back instantly.

"I can't, Agnivesh. We have reached an impasse and reiterating the same thing won't change anything except raising my blood pressure," she tried to joke.

"Okay, I won't. But promise me that you will at least let me take care of you."

"Only till the baby is born. Yes," she said, and he nodded. He was ready to take anything she was willing to give him at the moment, even though it was just a minuscule of what he wanted from her. He had almost eight months to persuade her, and he was determined to put his heart and soul into to make her realize that he loved her.

***

# All About Sona

8 June, 2012

*Dear Diary,*

*This may sound melodramatic, but I can't live without Sona, and the thought that I may never see her again torments me every second. I haven't slept a wink in the last few days. I have even tried to knock myself out with alcohol, but it is of no use. It's been almost fifteen days now since that incident, and I haven't seen her since then. I wait for her outside the sports complex every day, but she never turns up. I went to her college too to catch a glimpse of her, but she didn't come there either. I called her, I messaged her, I begged her, I even threatened her through messages, but nothing worked and then she blocked me. I did see Gayatri in college, and I gathered the courage one day to ask her about Sona. I know she doesn't like me, but I had no other way to know about Sona. Initially, she didn't tell me anything about her, but after my incessant requests, she agreed to talk to me about her. She told me that she met with an accident two weeks before, and lost her grandfather the same day too. That is the reason why she hasn't been coming to college.*

*So this is how she has explained the bruises that I gave her. She lied that she met with an accident. She hasn't shared that incident with anyone, not even Gayatri.*

*Gayatri has turned a little softer towards me since then. Perhaps, she has recognized that I truly care for Sona. She has made a plan to reunite me with Sona. Gayatri is getting engaged tomorrow, and she has invited me too. She told me that she has convinced Sona to attend her engagement and that I can meet her there. So tomorrow, I will hopefully be meeting her. I will beg her to forgive me, and if she doesn't, I will leave this world in the hope to see her again in the next life. I can't live with this pain anymore. I know I must let her go, I am no good for her, but I can't. Call me selfish here, but I am going to try till my last breath. So tomorrow, she will either come back to my life, or I will end my life.*

~

# 17

**Five Months Later**

A solemn drop of grief welled up in Reeva's eyes and tickled her cheeks as she read the last page of Kartik's diary. She closed the diary and kept it over her swollen belly. One-sided love is also a kind of disease that kills your ability to comprehend, because the reality is that one-sided love evokes the need to have your love acknowledged, without realizing that you can never force the other person to feel the same way for you. She couldn't change what had already happened. She couldn't bring Kartik back no matter how much she lamented, but she could surely make peace with her past by forgiving him. That was the only thing that Kartik had wanted. Her forgiveness.

In the past five months, she had picked up the diary to read many times, but could never gather enough courage to go down that lane again. But that day, she had an insight that she needed to finish the uncompleted chapters of her life so that she might begin writing a new one. She leaned her head back on the headrest of her bed and looked up at the luxurious ceiling of her room. She traced the circular pattern of the concealed lighting with her eyes. It was around midnight and she was dead tired because of all the gruelling work at her workshop. Still, sleep evaded her. Her business had grown ten fold in the past few months, especially after the collaboration of *Kreative Krafts* with a leading event planner in the city. Because of that, she had to employ new people for the job.

Agnivesh had renovated her workshop and upgraded it ergonomically, despite her disapproval of it.

'I am the owner of this place, and I want to renovate it. Do you have a problem with that? You may change the place if you wish,' he had countered then. She could have shifted from that place, but she knew that Agnivesh would buy the new place too. Reeva smiled ruminating over their fight about this. She knew that he was doing it all for her. He had dedicated every second of his life to her since then. He had even dragged her to this lavish new flat from that room at her workshop, saying that he was doing it for his baby. She couldn't say no as she had promised him that she would let him take care of her until the baby...babies were born.

She came to know that she was carrying twins on her first ultrasound. Knowing that, she had cried and laughed at the same time. She was happy that now she would be able to have one kid for herself, but also scared of how she would do it without any support from her family. This was another reason why she was letting Agnivesh take care of her.

He hadn't left her alone even for a day since then. He cancelled all his meetings that demanded him to leave the city. He shifted his main office from Mumbai to Surat. He also stayed at the same flat with her. She couldn't refuse it, because he never asked for her permission. He did everything in his power to undo that one wrong he had done to her. He got her name cleared from the police records. He even admitted the truth in front of her parents. Reeva shuddered upon recalling how angry her father got, knowing that Agnivesh had been the reason behind all her sufferings.

And the fact that Reeva was supporting Agnivesh in front of her parents got her father even more riled up. She was still engrossed in her thoughts when she felt a firm kick in her stomach. It was so intense that the diary slid down her belly instantly. She was in her sixth month and had felt a fluttering inside her stomach many a times, but this was the first time she was experiencing a kick. Her stomach roiled and a side of her belly bumped up, then bounced rapidly. It freaked her out. This was the first time she was witnessing something like this.

"Agnivesh!" she yelled at the top of her voice. Agnivesh rushed to her side instantly. Panic gushed through his gut as he saw her face etched with worry. Even though they were both living in the same house, she had never called out to him for help. "What's wrong?" He sat beside her and caressed her cheek. "Something is happening inside my belly. It's freaking me out," she said, and her stomach bounced in an arrhythmic manner again.

"See, I guess they are fighting inside. Shall we go to the doctor?" she said, and her stomach roiled again.

"I guess it's normal. They are growing. Just calm down," he tried to appease her.

"How do you know?" she asked.

"Because I have been reading a lot of pregnancy guidebooks lately. Shall I bring you something to eat?" he asked to divert her mind.

"Yes, I guess they are hungry. I will get something on my own." She started to get up, but Agnivesh motioned her to remain seated. Soon, he was back with a bowl of yoghurt. Reeva finished the bowl, while he kept watching her with pure adoration. "You scared me," he said.

"Did I? Even I was scared. It felt like a whirlwind in my stomach," she said, keeping the bowl aside. He snickered, "I thought you had the nightmare again."

“Nah. I don’t have them anymore,” she said, trying to remember the last time she had had one of them. “I don’t even remember when I had it last. I guess, I haven’t had any since I came to know about my pregnancy,” she added.

“Or since you confronted the cause of the nightmares,” he said, and Reeva looked at him confused. “You had kept everything suppressed inside you, thereby that traumatic experience was acting like a trigger. Once you let everything out, you got rid of them. A wound can never heal if it still contains the prickle,” he added.

We assume that pretending everything is fine will solve the problem, but the reality is that everything can never be fine until one isn’t fine from the inside. For that, it’s important to let go of the things you can’t change. Perhaps, Agnivesh was right. It was all because somewhere she held herself responsible for what had happened, and the day she realized that she had been punished for the same, her conscience made peace with her mind. Her trance was broken when she felt the kicks and jabs in her stomach again. She gasped and her hands flew to her belly.

“May I feel it?” asked Agnivesh, looking at her with pleading eyes. She nodded, smiling at him. She had maintained her distance with Agnivesh all this while; rather, this was the longest conversation—besides the fights—that they had had in the last few months. But in that moment, she felt like he deserved to experience this feeling. He placed his hands timidly over her belly, dreading that he shouldn’t hurt her or the kids. He felt a ball-like movement under his hands, and then a kick and then another one.

“Oh God! They are actually fighting,” he said.

“I think your kid has beaten mine,” she said, feigning anger. They both laughed while their eyes glossed with tears. It seemed so normal, just like any other couple anticipating the birth of their children. But were they? No. They were far from being a normal couple. He was living with regret, while she was living under an obligation. He had devoted himself to her just to undo that one wrongdoing he had done to her, while she was sacrificing a piece of her heart just to give him back what he had lost because of her. They were unaware of how much they needed each other. He looked wistfully at her and then whispered the same thing the umpteenth time, "Let's do it together, Reeva. Instead of calling them your kid and mine, let's call them ours."

"We *are* doing it together, Agnivesh, but only till they are born. We aren't meant to be together. So the day they are born, we will part our ways," she replied. She had thought about it so many times, and she had come up with the same conclusion each time, that even if they did forgive each other, they would still consider each other the culprit at the back of their minds. And any relationship built on adjustments and compromises could never flourish the way it should. So, in her opinion, it was better to part ways rather than live together and curse each other.

He didn't say anything in response. He never pushed Reeva, but made sure to remind her from time to time that no matter how many times she said *no*, he would still be waiting for her.

***

# 18

**Three months later**

Agnivesh couldn't take his eyes off of her angelic face. She had closed her eyes and her eyelids were a little swollen. Her chest was heaving in rhythm with her soft breathing. The sight in front of him had captivated him so much that he didn't even care to acknowledge anything else around him. His hand trembled as he slowly reached out to touch the curve of her soft cheek. He ran the back of his finger gently across her face, and his body tingled with ecstasy. His eyes welled up with tears of glee when she responded to his touch with a smile. In that moment, the world seemed to have stopped around him. How did he get so lucky to hold her in his arms! The smile that had just touched her lips told him that she had forgiven him and accepted him with all her heart. He brought his face down to brush his lips on her forehead.

"Mine," he whispered against her forehead and grazed his lips slightly. He saw her lips curling up in a smile again. Pure and divine. She tried to open her eyes, but shut them back instantly. Maybe the light was too bright for her. He brushed his finger gently against the soft pad of her palm, and she immediately curled her tiny fingers around his finger.

"Congratulations, Mr. Solanki," the nurse snapped him out of his daze, and he looked at the nurse dumbfounded, as if he hadn't even been aware of her presence.

"Congratulations to you for your daughter," she repeated.

"Thanks," he smiled and looked back at the pink bundle of bliss that the nurse had just handed him. He was standing outside the operation theatre. There had been a few complications because of which the doctor had to operate on Reeva.

*Reeva.*

Her name buzzed in his mind and he snapped his gaze back to the nurse.

"How is Reeva...and my second child?"

"Reeva is fine, but still unconscious. And here is your second baby." Another nurse came out of the operation theatre with a baby wrapped in a blue blanket in her arms. His eyes instantly gleamed with pride. He held his daughter in the cradle of one of his arms, and extended the other hand to hold baby number two.

"It's a boy," the nurse said, carefully handing over the baby to him. His chest swelled with joy, and he felt like the richest man in the world.

"Shall I take them back?" the nurse asked Agnivesh, and his grip around the babies stiffened in reflex. "Why?" he asked.

"We need to keep them in the nursery for some time. It's for preventive care," she elucidated. He looked at her incredulously.

"It's important for them, Mr. Solanki. Don't worry, we will take care of them," she assured, and he hesitantly let her take them away. The moment they were gone, he started pining to have them in his arms again, as if he had known them for ages.

"When can I meet Reeva?" he asked the other nurse.

"As soon as she gets shifted to her room."

"Did Reeva see them?" he shot another question.

"Just the glimpse," she smiled at him.

Half an hour later, he found himself standing outside the room where Reeva had just got shifted into. He wanted to go in and see her, but found himself in a quandary. What if she refused to meet him? She had permitted him to look after her for only as long as she carried the babies. What if she didn't want to see him now? Keeping all his perturbations aside, he stepped into the room. He relaxed when he found her sleeping. She was dressed in the hospital gown and one of her hands had the IV drip injected into it. There was a slight swelling on her face, but she looked relaxed. He sat on a chair perched beside the bed and slowly slid his hand into her free hand.

"I don't know what I should say or do to make you realize that I need you. I have just witnessed the biggest joy of my life, holding my kids in my arms. And even imagining that it will end soon, chills my spine. I need you, Reeva, and I need my kids, both of them. I can't let you go. You know, I was afraid to face you today because I know that our deal ends here, and I will have no right anymore to foist myself on you. But I want you to know that I need you in my life. Forever." He stopped as he saw her swallow. Her nostrils flared and the sides of her eyes moistened. A clear sign that she wasn't asleep. She had been listening to him, yet she didn't push him away. He felt hopeful at that moment.

"Open your eyes, Reeva, and tell me that you want us as much as I want you. I know there will be hurdles, but we will conquer them together. Wake up, Reeva, I know you aren't sleeping," he said, and she squeezed her eyes tighter.

Before she could answer him, Reeva's parents entered the room. They had been keeping their distance since Reeva had started living with Agnivesh without marriage. They were against it, and Reeva knew that they would never understand her situation. But today, when Agnivesh informed them of the birth of their twins, they couldn't stop themselves.

"Congratulations, you are grandparents now," Reeva said in an attempt to break the awkwardness, looking at her parents.

"Congratulations to you too…to both of you," corrected Sumitra instantly. She looked at Reeva wistfully and then whispered, "You are a mom now."

"Yes. Finally. Even though no one wanted me to be," Reeva said, nodding.

"We weren't against your motherhood, Reeva. It's just that we wanted it after the wedlock," Prakash said, standing beside his wife.

"Leave it. It's the time to celebrate. No bitter talks. All we want now is for you two to get married," Sumitra said, and Agnivesh looked at Reeva instantly to see her response. She just turned her head the other side.

"Reeva, don't tell me you are still thinking about not doing it. If not for yourself, think about your kids. What kind of a life will they get without—" Sumitra started, but Agnivesh held his hand up to stop her. He took Reeva's hand in his and said, "Don't think about the kids, Reeva, neither about me or your parents or the society. Just think about yourself and tell me what *you* want. I swear on my kids today that if you still don't want me, I will never show you my face again. Do you want me to go?" he asked.

This question hit a chord in Reeva's heart. Did she want him to go? No. Did she not want to see him ever again? Damn! How would she breathe if he were no longer around?

"Answer me once, Reeva. Do you want me gone forever?"

"No. I want you. I need you," she said, and her body shook with sobs. She winced at the pain of labour that still lingered in her body.

"Just calm down," Agnivesh soothed her, caressing her forehead. "I am not going anywhere, neither am I letting you go back on your words now," he said, lifting her hand up and kissing it.

***

# Epilogue

**Present day**

"And the award for the Emerging Entrepreneur of the Year goes to Ms. Reeva Panchal," announced the host and Reeva started walking towards the podium. The whole auditorium reverberated with the sound of claps as she received the award. Agnivesh's chest surged with pride for her. He planted a kiss on his daughter's head, who started squealing the moment she saw her mother on stage, while his son kept staring at his sister from his grandmother's lap.

"She is such an inspiration. At the age when most of us don't even have a clear vision about our future, she left her studies to follow her dream. She was just nineteen when she found her inner calling and fought against all odds to get there. And today, she has achieved what she wanted in life. Now, I'll request Ms. Reeva to share her inspiring journey of a successful entrepreneur with all of us here. I know many aspirants here who would love to hear about your struggles being a woman and how you overcame them. It will definitely motivate and guide them to chase their dreams," the host announced and requested Reeva to come to the dais. The auditorium roared with claps once again as she took the mike to speak. Agnivesh knew exactly what she was going to speak as she had been practicing her thank you speech for the last two days, but he frowned upon hearing her words when she started. This wasn't what she had planned to say.

"I am a firm believer that one must seek inspiration within, because the inspiration you get externally is short lived. It may ignite the fire, but it's your willpower that keeps you going. You may call my life inspiring because you are only aware of the end results. But trust me, if you peep inside, all you will see is *mess*. A complete mess. And the story that my dear friend"—she gestured towards the host—"just narrated about me is not true. I am a very simple girl and have done nothing inspiring that could motivate anyone. But yes, I do have my own share of experiences that I can share with you all, so that you may learn from the mistakes I made in my life.

"We all have flaws. We all make blunders. Nothing is mortifying in admitting that. Just keep one thing in your mind that when you make a mistake, be responsible for your actions and be prepared for the consequences. Learn from your mistakes, but never let yourself dwell on them. Life is beautiful and worth living. It can make you feel blissful, even when you are going through pain. Never hesitate to give it another chance, even if it causes you your umpteenth failure."

"There were times when on impulse, I concluded that I had no one who understood me, and hence shut myself down. But in retrospect now, I realize that I am so blessed to have people around me who love me with their heart and soul." Reeva looked at the row where her parents, her husband and her eleven-month-old kids were seated. Both the babies started squealing and banging their fists as they caught sight of their mother. Reeva blew a kiss towards them upon seeing them so excited. "My parents, my husband and my kids, Anay and Anaya, and another person who loved me more than his life. And the fact is, it was I who failed to understand them. All of them."

Reeva continued, addressing her parents this time, "Maa, Daddy, I know I have never been a good daughter, and I really regret all that I have made you go through. You were the ones who bore the brunt of my actions. You sacrificed your dreams and desires for your family, and I feel bad that I couldn't do the same for you. You sacrificed thinking that you would live out your dream through me one day, and I couldn't understand that. But trust me, I never wanted to hurt you. I was trying to pursue your dreams only...but just in my own way. I am sorry I couldn't make you understand that before. I always ran away and never tried to make you two a part of my inner-most self. You must be surprised why I am bringing it up now all of a sudden. It's because I am a mother now too, and I can't imagine my kids doing the same thing to me, hiding their problems, not discussing their fears and not letting me be a part of their dreams." She felt wistful as she saw her mother dabbing a handkerchief over her eyes. She continued, but addressing the audience this time, "Live your dream, breath your dream, go crazy over it...but in the pursuit of its fulfilment, never forget the ones who sacrificed their dreams for you." She caught Agnivesh's gaze, and he felt his stomach drop. She held pure adoration for him in her eyes.

"After a tragic incident in my life, I confined myself within a sheath and did not let anyone break those imaginary walls. Then one day, someone entered into my life and broke the armor, not to hurt me, but to heal me...and to heal himself too. Agnivesh, I really can't thank you enough for loving me the way I am without expecting anything in return. You taught me to love selflessly."

She continued again, addressing the audience, "Never deny yourself the pleasure of falling in love. It's beautiful. And never be afraid to fail in love. Trust me, failing in love is equally beautiful. If the former takes you up to new heights, the latter teaches you the important lessons of life. Love someone with all your heart and soul, but never more than your own life. I had a person in my life who loved me more than himself, and…" she trailed off for a moment, but soon pulled herself back together.

"The day he was gone, many lives were shattered. So do fall in love, but not more than with yourself. It may sound like rambling to many of you, but this is all I wanted to say. I won't bury my emotions anymore. I am going to end it here with just one sentence: Be your own inspiration and make your mistakes. Failure is your teacher, not the enemy. Thank you."

She ended the speech and the auditorium thundered with the sound of claps again. As she walked back to her seat, Agnivesh stood up, handing the baby over to Prakash. He opened his arms to hug Reeva, and she sprinted to grab the opportunity.

"It was beautiful. I am so proud of you. You did it," he said, enveloping her in his arms.

"We did it," she said, looking up at him. He was about to say something when she cut him off, "I love you. Let's get married."

He looked back and forth in her eyes, dumbfounded. "We are already married."

"We are, but I am yet to be your bride," she blushed and Agnivesh couldn't stop himself from kissing her forehead.

**END**

# Acknowledgement

It's impossible for me to start anything providential without remembering my grandparents. Whatever little wisdom and humility I have in me is all because of them.

My heartfelt thanks to my father-in-law, my parents and my nani ji for their endless love and blessings. Anita Vatsal, always, not only for this but for everything I am today. Ritu di, Nitasha, Richa for always encouraging me with their positive words. Anita, Pragti and Priti for being my emotional succor when I was anxious and frustrated.

My sincere thanks to team Invincible for making this happen, especially Mr. Ajay Setia, my editor Aditi Saxena and Ruchika Khanna.

My deep gratitude to all my relatives and friends for teaching me the invaluable lessons of life that helped me in portraying the characters. I can't mention all the names here, but you all know how blessed I feel to have you in my life.

People always ask me how I manage to write with two kids around, and the reason is that I am blessed with the sweetest and most supportive kids in the world, Agastya and Advitya.

And lastly, Amol Malik, nothing would have been possible without you. I really can't thank you enough for letting me spread my wings and follow my dreams.

# Author's Note

***Failure and mistakes are my true friends.***

***I never welcomed them.***

***I cried on their arrival.***

***I even cursed my fate because of them.***

***Yet, they left the life-altering lessons for me.***

A special thanks to you for reading this story. I will wait for your reviews, short or long doesn't matter, but do post them. You may connect with me:


Facebook: www.facebook.com/anjum.a.malik

Instagram: @anjumawasthi

Twitter: @anjum_awasthi

Email: anjumawasthi@gmail.com

## Also by the author

**The Twist of Fate**

**BLURB**

A young and vivacious girl, Raahi is all set to live her dream in a big city. A cruel twist of fate and her world starts collapsing around her. Aadit, a business analyst in New York, is effervescent and full of life. Or at least that's what he shows to the world, but deep down he is still struggling with his own demons. The fate interweaves their lives together and just when a bond is about to bloom, life throws another curve at them. They start drifting apart completely oblivious to what fate has in store for them. The Twist of Fate is a heartfelt and enamored tale of the entangled emotions of love that promises to keep your eyes glued to its pages.

**PROLOGUE**

Not bothering to wait for the elevator, I started climbing up the stairs of my office. The upheaval going in my mind had affected me to such an extent that I didn't even bother to return the greetings of my colleagues on the way to my cubicle.

"Are you okay?" asked Ankita, peering from the cubicle diagonally opposite to mine as I dropped my handbag on my table.

"Yeah," I lied, because at this moment I was anything but all right.

"Well, all the best for your first presentation," she smiled before resuming to type on her laptop.

*My first presentation...*

This was the last thing on my mind at the moment. Life is erratic and the most unpredictable thing. It never goes the way we plan. It was still hard to believe that it had taken just a week for my life to shatter to bits.

*Why me? Dammit, why me?*

I had always embraced whatever life offered me with my arms wide open and I was content with what I had. However, it wasn't like my life was all bed of roses; I had had my own share of miseries and maybe that was the reason I wasn't ready to accept what was now happening in my life. I had always been possessive when it came to my things, perhaps this was the reason why I found myself teetering on the brink of an abyss. It was something I just couldn't let go, period.

I felt my legs wobbling and hands trembling as I pulled my phone out of my handbag. I knew that nothing could recuperate my condition until I got to know what was going on in his life, for which it was important to talk to Dev—his roommate. He was the only person I could rely on at this moment. I called Dev with a gaggle of queries hovering in my mind. He rejected my call. I called him again and just as the last attempt, he cut my call off in first ring. Now why the hell was he avoiding me? Why was everyone around me on a mission to test my patience? I was stopped short from calling again when his message popped in: **I'm in a meeting. Will call you shortly.**

My presentation with my manager was due over the next hour. I prayed for Dev to call me before that, dreading the restlessness which otherwise threatened to mess with my concentration over my first presentation. I kept my phone aside and waited for his call. Why does it happen that a few seconds seem like an eternity when you are frenziedly waiting for something to happen? I kept checking my phone every few seconds, but nothing appeared on my notification bar. It was getting hard to curb the urge to call him again, but I restrained myself...*somehow*, as I didn't want to come across as some frantic girlfriend stalking her boyfriend.

It had been fifty-one minutes since his message had popped in, but still I didn't get any call from him. Clenching my phone in hand, I made my way to the washroom. I felt a certain heaviness in my chest and dryness in my sleep- deprived eyes. As I entered the freshly cleaned washroom, the smell of disinfectant made me nauseous. Covering my nose and mouth, I stood in front of the washbasin. The pale, fragile and sullen reflection that I saw in the huge mirror mounted on the wall in front of me, looked anything but me.

If just two weeks ago, when I first came to Noida, someone had told me that my image in the mirror would look like this, I would never have believed them.

"Why are you doing this to me?" my aching heart asked, hoping for it to reach him.

"Why are you letting him do this to you?" my subconscious snarled, pointing back at me. And I stood there... *numb*, as a silent tear peeped over the brim of my eye.

Printed by Libri Plureos GmbH in Hamburg,
Germany

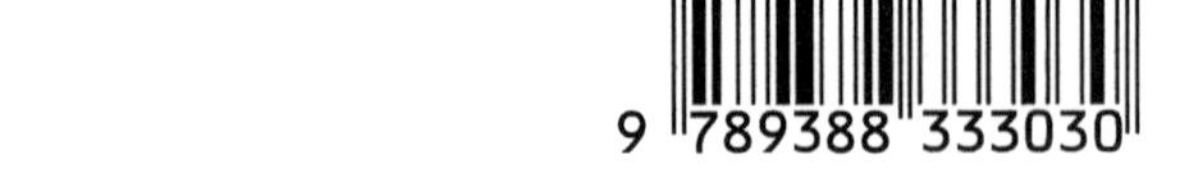